EARLY BRITAIN

CONTENTS

PREFACE.

This little book is an attempt to give a brief sketch of Britain under the early English conquerors, rather from the social than from the political point of view. For that purpose not much has been said about the doings of kings and statesmen; but attention has been mainly directed towards the less obvious evidence afforded us by existing monuments as to the life and mode of thought of the people themselves. The principal object throughout has been to estimate the importance of those elements in modern British life which are chiefly due to purely English or Low-Dutch influences.

The original authorities most largely consulted have been, first and above all, the "English Chronicle," and to an almost equal extent, Bæda's "Ecclesiastical History." These have been supplemented, where necessary, by Florence of Worcester and the other Latin writers of later date. I have not thought it needful, however, to repeat any of the gossiping stories from William of Malmesbury, Henry of Huntingdon, and their compeers, which make up the bulk of our early history as told in most modern books. Still less have I paid any attention to the romances of Geoffrey of Monmouth. Gildas, Nennius, and the other Welsh tracts have been sparingly employed, and always with a reference by name. Asser has been used with caution, where his information seems to be really contemporary. I have also derived some occasional hints from the old British bards, from *Beowulf*, from the laws, and from the charters in the "Codex Diplomaticus." These written documents have been helped out by some personal study of the actual early English relics preserved in various museums, and by the indirect evidence of local nomenclature.

Among modern books, I owe my acknowledgments in the first and highest degree to Dr. E.A. Freeman, from whose great and just authority, however, I have occasionally ventured to differ in some minor matters. Next, my acknowledgments are due to Canon Stubbs, to Mr. Kemble, and to Mr. J.R. Green. Dr. Guest's valuable papers in the Transactions of the Archæological Institute have supplied many useful suggestions. To Lappenberg and Sir Francis Palgrave I am also indebted for various details. Professor Rolleston's contributions to "Archæologia," as well as his Appendix to Canon Greenwell's "British Barrows," have been consulted for anthropological and antiquarian points; on which also Professor Huxley and Mr. Akerman have published useful papers. Professor Boyd Dawkins's work on "Early Man in Britain," as well as the writings of Worsaae and Steenstrup have helped in elucidating the condition of the English at the date of the Conquest. Nor must I forget the aid derived from Mr. Isaac Taylor's "Words and Places," from Professor Henry Morley's "English Literature," and from Messrs. Haddan and Stubbs' "Councils." To Mr. Gomme, Mr. E.B. Tylor, Mr. Sweet, Mr. James Collier, Dr. H. Leo, and perhaps others, I am under various obligations; and if any acknowledgments have been overlooked, I trust the injured person will forgive me when I have had already to quote so many authorities for so small a book. The popular character of the work renders it undesirable to load the pages with footnotes of reference; and scholars will generally see for themselves the source of the information given in the text.

Personally, my thanks are due to my friend, Mr. York Powell, for much valuable aid and assistance, and to the Rev. E. McClure, one of the Society's secretaries, for his kind revision of the volume in proof, and for several suggestions of which I have gladly availed myself.

As various early English names and phrases occur throughout the book, it will be best, perhaps, to say a few words about their pronunciation here, rather than to leave over that subject to the chapter on the Anglo-Saxon language, near the close of the work. A few notes on this matter are therefore appended below.

The simple vowels, as a rule, have their continental pronunciation, approximately thus: *â* as in *father*, *ă* as in *ask*; *ç* as in *there*, *ĕ* as in *men*; *î* as in *marine*, *ĭ* as *fit*; *ô* as in *note*, *ŏ* as in *not*; *ŭ* as in *brute*, *ŏ* as in *full*; **ȳ** as in *grün* (German), *ў* as in *hübsch* (German). The quantity of the vowels is not marked in this work. *Æ* is not a diphthong, but a simple vowel sound, the same as our own short *a* in *man*, *that*, &c. *Ea* is pronounced like *ya*. *C* is always hard, like *k*; and *g* is also always hard, as in *begin*: they must *never* be pronounced like *s* or *j*. The other consonants have the same values as in modern English. No vowel or consonant is ever mute. Hence we get the following approximate pronunciations: Ælfred and Æthelred, as if written Alfred and Athelred; Æthelstan and Dunstan, as Athelstahn and Doonstahn; Eadwine and Oswine, nearly as Yahd-weena and Ose-weena; Wulfsige and Sigeberht, as Wolf-seeg-a and Seeg-a-bayrt; Ceolred and Cynewulf, as Keole-red and Küne-wolf. These approximations look a little absurd when written down in the only modern phonetic equivalents; but that is the fault of our own existing spelling, not of the early English names themselves.

G.A.

11

CHAPTER I.

THE ORIGIN OF THE ENGLISH.

At a period earlier than the dawn of written history there lived somewhere among the great table-lands and plains of Central Asia a race known to us only by the uncertain name of Aryans. These Aryans were a fair-skinned and well-built people, long past the stage of aboriginal savagery, and possessed of a considerable degree of primitive culture. Though mainly pastoral in habit, they were acquainted with tillage, and they grew for themselves at least one kind of cereal grain. They spoke a language whose existence and nature we infer from the remnants of it which survive in the tongues of their descendants, and from these remnants we are able to judge, in some measure, of their civilisation and their modes of thought. The indications thus preserved for us show the Aryans to have been a simple and fierce community of early warriors, farmers, and shepherds, still in a partially nomad condition, living under a patriarchal rule, originally ignorant of all metals save gold, but possessing weapons and implements of stone,[1] and worshipping as their chief god the open heaven. We must not regard them as an idyllic and peaceable people: on the contrary, they were the fiercest and most conquering tribe ever known. In mental power and in plasticity of manners, however, they probably rose far superior to any race then living, except only the Semitic nations of the Mediterranean coast.

From the common Central Asian home, colonies of warlike Aryans gradually dispersed themselves, still in the pre-historic period, under pressure of population or hostile invasion, over many districts of Europe and Asia. Some of them moved southward, across the passes of Afghanistan, and occupied the fertile plains of the Indus and the Ganges, where they became the ancestors of the Brahmans and other modern high-caste Hindoos. The language which they took with them to their new settlements beyond the Himalayas was the Sanskrit, which still remains to this day the nearest of all dialects that we now possess to the primitive Aryan speech. From it are derived the chief modern tongues of northern India, from the Vindhyas to the Hindu Kush. Other Aryan tribes settled in the mountain districts west of Hindustan; and yet others found themselves a home in the hills of Iran or Persia, where they still preserve an allied dialect of the ancient mother tongue.

But the mass of the emigrants from the Central Asian fatherland moved further westward in successive waves, and occupied, one after another, the midland plains and mountainous peninsulas of Europe. First of all, apparently, came the Celts, who spread slowly across the South of Russia and Germany, and who are found at the dawn of authentic history extending over the entire western coasts and islands of the continent, from Spain to Scotland. Mingled in many places with the still earlier non-Aryan aborigines—perhaps Iberians and Euskarians, a short and swarthy race, armed only with weapons of polished stone, and represented at the present day by the Basques of the Pyrenees and the Asturias—the Celts held rule in Spain, Gaul, and Britain, up to the date of the several Roman conquests. A second great wave of Aryan immigration, that of the Hellenic and Italian races, broke over the shores of the *Ægean* and the Adriatic, where their cognate languages have become familiar to us in the two extreme and typical forms of the classical Greek and Latin. A third wave was that of the Teutonic or German people, who followed and drove out the Celts over a large part of central and western Europe; while a fourth and final swarm was that of the Slavonic tribes, which still inhabit only the extreme eastern portion of the continent.

With the Slavonians we shall have nothing to do in this enquiry; and with the Greek and Italian races we need only deal very incidentally. But the Celts, whom the English invaders found in possession of all Britain when they began their settlements in the island, form the subject of another volume in this series, and will necessarily call for some small portion of our attention here also; while it is to the Germanic race that the English stock itself actually belongs, so that we must examine somewhat more closely the course of Germanic immigration through Europe, and the nature of the primitive Teutonic civilisation.

The Germanic family of peoples consisted of a race which early split up into two great hordes or stocks, speaking dialects which differed slightly from one another through the action of the various circumstances to which they were each exposed. These two stocks are the High German and the Low German (with which last may be included the Gothic and the Scandinavian). Moving across Europe from east to west, they slowly drove out the Celts from Germany and the central plains, and took possession of the whole district between the Alps, the Rhine, and the Baltic, which formed their limits at the period when they first came into contact with the Roman power. The Goths, living in closest proximity to the empire, fell upon it during the decline and decay of Rome, settled in Italy, Gaul, and Spain, and becoming absorbed in the mass of the native population, disappear altogether from history as a distinguishable nationality. But the High and Low Germans retain to the present day their distinctive language and features; and the latter branch, to which the English people belong, still lives for the most part in the same lands which it has held ever since the date of the early Germanic immigration.

The Low Germans, in the third century after Christ, occupied in the main the belt of flat country between the Baltic and the mouths of the Rhine. Between them and the old High German Swabians lay a race intermediate in tongue and blood, the Franks. The Low Germans were divided, like most other barbaric races, into several fluctuating and ill-marked tribes, whose names are loosely and perhaps interchangeably

15

used by the few authorities which remain to us. We must not expect to find among them the definiteness of modern civilised nations, but rather such a vagueness as that which characterised the loose confederacies of North American Indians or the various shifting peoples of South Africa. But there are three of their tribes which stand fairly well marked off from one another in early history, and which bore, at least, the chief share in the colonisation of Britain. These three tribes are the Jutes, the English, and the Saxons. Closely connected with them, but less strictly bound in the same family tie, were the Frisians.

The Jutes, the northernmost of the three divisions, lived in the marshy forests and along the winding fjords of Jutland, the extreme peninsula of Denmark, which still preserves their name in our own day. The English dwelt just to the south, in the heath-clad neck of the peninsula, which we now call Sleswick. And the Saxons, a much larger tribe, occupied the flat continental shore, from the mouth of the Oder to that of the Rhine. At the period when history lifts the curtain upon the future Germanic colonists of Britain, we thus discover them as the inhabitants of the low-lying lands around the Baltic and the North Sea, and closely connected with other tribes on either side, such as the Frisians and the Danes, who still speak very cognate Low German and Scandinavian languages.

But we have not yet fully grasped the extent of the relationship between the first Teutonic settlers in Britain and their continental brethren. Not only are the true Englishmen of modern England distantly connected with the Franks, who never to our knowledge took part in the colonisation of the island at all; and more closely connected with the Frisians, some of whom probably accompanied the earliest piratical hordes; as well as with the Danes, who settled at a later date in all the northern counties: but they are also most closely connected of all with those members of the colonising tribes who did not themselves bear a share in the settlement, and whose descendants are still living in Denmark and in various parts of Germany. The English proper, it is true, seem to have deserted their old home in Sleswick in a body; so that, according to Bæda, the Christian historian of Northumberland, in his time this oldest England by the shores of the Baltic lay waste and unpeopled, through the completeness of the exodus. But the Jutes appear to have migrated in small numbers, while the larger part of the tribe remained at home in their native marshland; and of the more numerous Saxons, though a great swarm went out to conquer southern Britain, a vast body was still left behind in Germany, where it continued independent and pagan till the time of Karl the Great, long after the Teutonic colonists of Britain had grown into peaceable and civilised Christians. It is from the statements of later historians with regard to these continental Saxons that our knowledge of the early English customs and institutions, during the continental period of English history, must be mainly inferred. We gather our picture of the English and Saxons who first came to this country from the picture drawn for us of those among their brethren whom they left behind in the primitive English home.

These three tribes, the Jutes, the English, and the Saxons, had not yet, apparently, advanced far enough in the idea of national unity to possess a separate general name, distinguishing them altogether from the other tribes of the Germanic stock. Most probably they did not regard themselves at this period as a single nation at all, or even as more closely bound to one another than to the surrounding and kindred tribes. They may have united at times for purposes of a special war; but their union was merely analogous to that of two North American peoples, or two modern European nations, pursuing a common policy for awhile. At a later date, in Britain, the three tribes learned to call themselves collectively by the name of that one among them which earliest rose to supremacy—the English; and the whole southern half of the island came to be known by their name as England. Even from the first it seems probable that their language was spoken of as English only, and comparatively little as Saxon. But since it would be inconvenient to use the name of one dominant tribe alone, the English, as equivalent to those of the three, and since it is desirable to have a common title for all the Germanic colonists of Britain, whenever it is necessary to speak of them together, we shall employ the late and, strictly speaking, incorrect form of "Anglo-Saxons" for this purpose. Similarly, in order to distinguish the earliest pure form of the English language from its later modern form, now largely enriched and altered by the addition of Romance or Latin words and the disuse of native ones, we shall always speak of it, where distinction is necessary, as Anglo-Saxon. The term is now too deeply rooted in our language to be again uprooted; and it has, besides, the merit of supplying a want. At the same time, it should be remembered that the expression Anglo-Saxon is purely artificial, and was never used by the people themselves in describing their fellows or their tongue. When they did not speak of themselves as Jutes, English, and Saxons respectively, they spoke of themselves as English alone.

1. Professor Boyd Dawkins has shown that the Continental Celts were still in their stone age when they invaded Europe; whence we must conclude that the original Aryans were unacquainted with the use of bronze.

* * * * *

CHAPTER II.

THE ENGLISH BY THE
SHORES OF THE BALTIC.

From the notices left us by Bæda in Britain, and by Nithard and others on the continent, of the habits and manners which distinguished those Saxons who remained in the old fatherland, we are able to form some idea of the primitive condition of those other Saxons, English, and Jutes, who afterwards colonized Britain, during the period while they still all lived together in the heather-clad wastes and marshy lowlands of Denmark and Northern Germany. The early heathen poem of *Beowulf* also gives us a glimpse of their ideas and their mode of thought. The known physical characteristics of the race, the nature of the country which they inhabited, the analogy of other Germanic tribes, and the recent discoveries of pre-historic archæology, all help us to piece out a fairly consistent picture of their appearance, their manner of life, and their rude political institutions.

We must begin by dismissing from our minds all those modern notions which are almost inevitably implied by the use of language directly derived from that of our heathen ancestors, but now mixed up in our conceptions with the most advanced forms of European civilisation. We must not allow such words as "king" and "English" to mislead us into a species of filial blindness to the real nature of our Teutonic forefathers. The little community of wild farmers and warriors who lived among the dim woodlands of Sleswick, beside the swampy margin of the North

Sea, has grown into the nucleus of a vast empire, only very partially Germanic in blood, and enriched by all the alien culture of Egypt, Assyria, Greece, and Rome. But as it still preserves the identical tongue of its early barbarous days, we are naturally tempted to read our modern acquired feelings into the simple but familiar terms employed by our continental predecessors. What the early English called a king we should now-a-days call a chief; what they called a meeting of wise men we should now-a-days call a palaver. In fact, we must recollect that we are dealing with a purely barbaric race—not savage, indeed, nor without a certain rude culture of its own, the result of long centuries of previous development; yet essentially military and predatory in its habits, and akin in its material civilisation to many races which we now regard as immeasurably our inferiors. If we wish for a modern equivalent of the primitive Anglo-Saxon level of culture, we may perhaps best find it in the Kurds of the Turkish and Persian frontier, or in the Mahrattas of the wild mountain region of the western Deccan.

The early English in Sleswick and Friesland had partially reached the agricultural stage of civilisation. They tilled little plots of ground in the forest; but they depended more largely for subsistence upon their cattle, and they were also hunters and trappers in the great belts of woodland or marsh which everywhere surrounded their isolated villages. They were acquainted with the use of bronze from the first period of their settlement in Europe, and some of the battle-axes or shields which they manufactured from this metal were beautifully chased with exquisite decorative patterns, equalling in taste the ornamental designs still employed by the Polynesian islanders. Such weapons, however, were doubtless intended for the use of the chieftains only, and were probably employed as insignia of rank alone. They are still discovered in the barrows which cover the remains of the early chieftains; though it is possible that they may really belong to the monuments of a yet earlier race. But iron was certainly employed by the English, at least, from about the first century of the Christian era, and its use was perhaps introduced into the marshlands of Sleswick by the Germanic conquerors of the north. Even at this early date, abundant proof exists of mercantile intercourse with the Roman world (probably through Pannonia), whereby the alien culture of the south was already engrafted in part upon the low civilisation of the native English. Amber was then exported from the Baltic, while gold, silver, and glass beads were given in return. Roman coins are discovered in Low German tombs of the first five centuries in Sleswick, Holstein, Friesland, and the Isles; and Roman patterns are imitated in the iron weapons and utensils of the same period. Gold byzants of the fifth century prove an intercourse with Constantinople at the exact date of the colonisation of Britain. From the very earliest moment when we catch a glimpse of its nature, the home-grown English culture had already begun to be modified by the superior arts of Rome. Even the alphabet was known and used in its Runic form, though the absence of writing materials caused its employment to be restricted to inscriptions on wooden tablets, on rude stone monuments, or on utensils of metal-work. A golden drinking-horn found in Sleswick, and engraved with the maker's name, referred to the middle of the fourth century, contains the earliest known specimen of the English language.

The early English society was founded entirely on the tie of blood. Every clan or family lived by itself and formed a guild for mutual protection, each kinsman being his brother's keeper, and bound to avenge his death by feud with the tribe or clan which had killed him. This duty of blood-revenge was the supreme religion of the race. Moreover, the clan was answerable as a whole for the ill-deeds of all its members; and the fine payable for murder or injury was handed over by the family of the wrong-doer to the family of the injured man.

Each little village of the old English community possessed a general independence of its own, and lay apart from all the others, often surrounded by a broad belt or mark of virgin forest. It consisted of a clearing like those of the American backwoods, where a single family or kindred had made its home, and preserved its separate independence intact. Each of these families was known by the name of its real or supposed ancestor, the patronymic being formed by the addition of the syllable *ing*. Thus the descendants of Ælla would be called Ællings, and their *ham* or stockade would be known as Ællingaham, or in modern form Allingham. So the *tun* or enclosure of the Culmings would be Culmingatun, similarly modernised into Culmington. Names of this type abound in the newer England at the present day; as in the case of Birmingham, Buckingham, Wellington, Kensington, Basingstoke, and Paddington. But while in America the clearing is merely a temporary phase, and the border of forest is soon cut down so as to connect the village with its neighbours, in the old Anglo-Saxon fatherland the border of woodland, heath, or fen was jealously guarded as a frontier and natural defence for the little predatory and agricultural community. Whoever crossed it was bound to give notice of his coming by blowing a horn; else he was cut down at once as a stealthy enemy. The marksmen wished to remain separate from all others, and only to mix with those of their own kin. In this primitive love of separation we have the germ of that local independence and that isolated private home life which is one of the most marked characteristics of modern Englishmen.

In the middle of the clearing, surrounded by a wooden stockade, stood the village, a group of rude detached huts. The marksmen each possessed a separate little homestead, consisting usually of a small wooden house or shanty, a courtyard, and a cattle-fold. So far, private property in land had already begun. But the forest and the pasture land were not appropriated: each man had a right from year to year to let loose his kine or horses on a certain equal or proportionate space of land assigned to him by the village in council. The wealth of the people consisted mainly in cattle which fed on the pasture, and pigs turned out to fatten on the acorns of the forest: but a small portion of the soil was ploughed and sown; and this portion also was distributed to the villagers for tillage by annual arrangement. The hall of the chief rose in the midst of the lesser houses, open to all comers. The village moot, or assembly of freemen, met in the open air, under some sacred tree, or beside some old monumental stone, often a relic of the older aboriginal race, marking the tomb of a dead chieftain, but worshipped as a god by the English immigrants. At these informal meetings, every head of a family had a right to appear and deliberate. The primitive English constitution was a pure republican aristocracy or oligarchy of householders, like that which still survives in the Swiss forest cantons.

But there were yet distinctions of rank in the villages and in the loose tribes formed by their union for purposes of war or otherwise. The people were divided into three classes of *æthelings* or chieftains, *freolings* or freemen, and *theows* or slaves. The *æthelings* were the nobles and rulers of each tribe. There was no king: but when the tribes joined together in a war, their *æthelings* cast lots together, and whoever drew the winning lot was made commander for the time being. As soon as the war was over, each tribe returned to its own independence. Indeed, the only really coherent body was the village or kindred: and the whole course of early English history consists of a long and tedious effort at increased national unity, which was never fully realised till the Norman conquerors bound the whole nation together in the firm grasp of William, Henry, and Edward.

In personal appearance, the primitive Anglo-Saxons were typical Germans of very unmixed blood. Tall, fair-haired, and gray-eyed, their limbs were large and stout, and their heads of the round or brachycephalic type, common to most Aryan races. They did not intermarry with other nations, preserving their Germanic blood pure and unadulterated. But as they had slaves, and as these slaves must in many cases have been captives spared in war, we must suppose that such descriptions apply, strictly speaking, to the freemen and chieftains alone. The slaves might be of any race, and in process of time they must have learnt to speak English, and their children must have become English in all but blood. Many of them, indeed, would probably be actually English on the father's side, though born of slave mothers. Hence we must be careful not to interpret the expressions of historians, who would be thinking of the free classes only, and especially of the nobles, as though they applied to the slaves as well. Wherever slavery exists, the blood of the slave community is necessarily very mixed. The picture which the heathen English have drawn of themselves in *Beowulf* is one of savage pirates, clad in shirts of ring-armour, and greedy of gold and ale. Fighting and drinking are their two delights. The noblest leader is he who builds a great hall, throws it open for his people to carouse in, and liberally deals out beer, and bracelets, and money at the feast. The joy of battle is keen in their breasts. The sea and the storm are welcome to them. They are fearless and greedy pirates, not ashamed of living by the strong hand alone.

In creed, the English were pagans, having a religion of beliefs rather than of rites. Their chief deity, perhaps, was a form of the old Aryan Sky-god, who took with them the guise of Thunor or Thunder (in Scandinavian, Thor), an angry warrior hurling his hammer, the thunder-bolt, from the stormy clouds. These thunder-bolts were often found buried in the earth; and being really the polished stone-axes of the earlier inhabitants, they do actually resemble a hammer in shape. But Woden, the special god of the Teutonic race, had practically usurped the highest place in their mythology: he is represented as the leader of the Germans in their exodus from Asia to north-western Europe, and since all the pedigrees of their chieftains were traced back to Woden, it is not improbable that he may have been really a deified ancestor of the principal Germanic families. The popular creed, however, was mainly one of lesser gods, such as elves, ogres, giants, and monsters, inhabitants of the mark and fen, stories of whom still survive in English villages as folk-lore or fairy tales. A few legends of the pagan time are preserved for us in Christian books. *Beowulf* is rich in allusions to these ancient superstitions. If we may build upon the slender materials which alone are available, it would seem that the dead chieftains were buried in barrows, and ghost-worship was practised at their tombs. The temples were mere stockades of wood, with rude blocks or monoliths to represent deities and altars. Probably their few rites consisted merely of human or other sacrifices to the gods or the ghosts of departed chiefs. There was a regular priesthood of the great gods, but each man was priest for his own household. As in most other heathen communities, the real worship of the people was mainly directed to the special family deities of every hearth. The great gods were appealed to by the chieftains and by the race in battle: but the household gods or deified ancestors received the chief homage of the churls by their own firesides.

Thus the Anglo-Saxons, before the great exodus from Denmark and North Germany, appear as a race of fierce, cruel, and barbaric pagans, delighting in the sea, in slaughter, and in drink. They dwelt in little isolated communities, bound together internally by ties of blood, and uniting occasionally with others only for purposes of rapine. They lived a life which mainly alternated between grazing, piratical seafaring, and cattle-lifting; always on the war-trail against the possessions of others, when they were not specially engaged in taking care of their own. Every record and every indication shows them to us as fiercer heathen prototypes of the Scotch clans in the most lawless days of the Highlands. Incapable of union for any peaceful purpose at home, they learned their earliest lesson of subordination in their piratical attacks upon the civilised Christian community of Roman Britain. We first meet with them in history in the character of destroyers and sea-robbers. Yet they possessed already in their wild marshy home the germs of those free institutions which have made the history of England unique amongst the nations of Europe.

* * * * *

CHAPTER III.

THE ENGLISH SETTLE IN BRITAIN.

Proximity to the sea turns robbers into corsairs. When predatory tribes reach the seaboard they always take to piracy, provided they have attained the shipbuilding level of culture. In the ancient Ægean, in the Malay Archipelago, in the China seas, we see the same process always taking place. Probably from the first period of their severance from the main Aryan stock in Central Asia, the Low German race and their ancestors had been a predatory and conquering people, for ever engaged in raids and smouldering warfare with their neighbours. When they reached the Baltic and the islands of the Frisian coast, they grew naturally into a nation of pirates. Even during the bronze age, we find sculptured stones with representations of long row-boats, manned by several oarsmen, and in one or two cases actually bearing a rude sail. Their prows and sterns stand high out of the water, and are adorned with intricate carvings. They seem like the predecessors of the long ships—snakes and sea-dragons—which afterwards bore the northern corsairs into every river of Europe. Such boats, adapted for long sea-voyages, show a considerable intercourse, piratical or commercial, between the Anglo-Saxon or Scandinavian North and other distant countries. Certainly, from the earliest days of Roman rule on the German Ocean to the thirteenth century, the Low Dutch and Scandinavian tribes carried on an almost unbroken course of expeditions by sea, beginning in every case with mere descents upon the coast for the purposes of plunder, but ending, as a rule, with regular colonisation or political supremacy. In this manner the people of the Baltic and the North Sea ravaged or settled in every country on the sea-shore, from Orkney, Shetland, and the Faroes, to Normandy, Apulia, and Greece; from Boulogne and Kent, to Iceland, Greenland, and, perhaps, America. The colonisation of South-Eastern Britain was but the first chapter in this long history of predatory excursions on the part of the Low German peoples.

The piratical ships of the early English were row-boats of very simple construction. We actually possess one undoubted specimen at the present day, whose very date is fixed for us by the circumstances of its discovery. It was dug up, some years since, from a peat-bog in Sleswick, the old England of our forefathers, along with iron arms and implements, and in association with Roman coins ranging in date from A.D. 67 to A.D. 217. It may therefore be pretty confidently assigned to the first half of the third century. In this interesting relic, then, we have one of the identical boats in which the descents upon the British coast were first made. The craft is rudely built of oaken boards, and is seventy feet long by nine broad. The stem and stern are alike in shape, and the boat is fitted for being beached upon the foreshore. A sculptured stone at Häggeby, in Uplande, roughly represents for us such a ship under way, probably of about the same date. It is rowed with twelve pairs of oars, and has no sails; and it contains no other persons but the rowers and a coxswain, who acted doubtless as leader of the expedition. Such a boat might convey about 120 fighting men.

There are some grounds for believing that, even before the establishment of the Roman power in Britain, Teutonic pirates from the northern marshlands were already in the habit of plundering the Celtic inhabitants of the country between the Wash and the mouth of the Thames; and it is possible that an English colony may, even then, have established itself in the modern Lincolnshire. But, be this as it may, we know at least that during the period of the Roman occupation, Low German adventurers were constantly engaged in descending upon the exposed coasts of the English Channel and the North Sea. The Low German tribe nearest to the Roman provinces was that of the Saxons, and accordingly these Teutonic pirates, of whatever race, were known as Saxons by the provincials, and all Englishmen are still so called by the modern Celts, in Wales, Scotland, and Ireland.

The outlying Roman provinces were close at hand, easy to reach, rich, ill-defended, and a tempting prey for the barbaric tribesmen of the north. Setting out in their light open skiffs from the islands at the mouth of the Elbe, or off the shore afterwards submerged in what is now the Zuyder Zee, the English or Saxon pirates crossed the sea with the prevalent north-east wind, and landed all along the provincial coasts of Gaul and Britain. As the empire decayed under the assaults of the Goths, their ravages turned into regular settlements. One great body pillaged, age after age, the neighbourhood of Bayeux, where, before the middle of the fifth century, it established a flourishing colony, and where the towns and villages all still bear names of Saxon origin. Another horde first plundered and then took up its abode near Boulogne, where local names of the English patronymic type also abound to the present day. In Britain itself, at a date not later than the end of the fourth century, we find (in the "Notitia Imperil") an officer who bears the title of Count of the Saxon Shore, and whose jurisdiction extended from Lincolnshire to Southampton Water. The title probably indicates that piratical incursions had already set in on Britain, and the duty of the count was most likely that of repelling the English invaders.

As soon as the Romans found themselves compelled to withdraw their garrison from Britain, leaving the provinces to defend themselves as best they might, the temptation to the English pirates became a thousand times stronger than before. Though the so-called history of the conquest, handed down to us by Bæda and the "English Chronicle,"[1] is now considered by many enquirers to be mythical in almost every particular, the facts themselves speak out for us with unhesitating certainty. We know that about the middle of the fifth century, shortly after the withdrawal of the regular Roman troops, several bodies of heathen Anglo-Saxons, belonging to the three tribes of Jutes, English, and Saxons, settled *en masse* on the south-eastern shores of Britain, from the Firth of Forth to the Isle of Wight. The age of mere plundering descents was decisively over, and the age of settlement and colonisation had set in. These heathen Anglo-Saxons drove away, exterminated, or enslaved the Romanised and Christianised Celts, broke down every vestige of Roman civilisation, destroyed the churches, burnt the villas, laid waste many of the towns, and re-introduced a long period of pagan barbarism. For a while Britain remains enveloped in an age of complete uncertainty, and heathen myths intervene between the Christian historical period of the Romans and the Christian historical period initiated by the conversion of Kent. Of South-Eastern Britain under the pagan Anglo-Saxons we know practically nothing, save by inference and analogy, or by the scanty evidence of archæology.

According to tradition the Jutes came first. In 449, says the Celtic legend (the date is quite untrustworthy), they landed in Kent, where they first settled in Ruim, which we English call Thanet—then really an island, and gradually spread themselves over the mainland, capturing the great Roman fortress of Rochester and coast land as far as London. Though the details of this story are full of mythical absurdities, the analogy of the later Danish colonies gives it an air of great probability, as the Danes always settled first in islands or peninsulas, and thence proceeded to overrun, and finally to annex, the adjacent district. A second Jutish horde established itself in the Isle of Wight and on the opposite shore of Hampshire. But the whole share borne by the Jutes in the settlement of Britain seems to have been but small.

The Saxons came second in time, if we may believe the legends. In 477, Ælle, with his three sons, is said to have landed on the south coast, where he founded the colony of the South Saxons, or Sussex. In 495, Cerdic and Cynric led another kindred horde to the south-western shore, and made the first settlement of the West Saxons, or Wessex. Of the beginnings of the East Saxon community in Essex, and of the Middle Saxons in Middlesex, we know little, even by tradition. The Saxons undoubtedly came over in large numbers; but a considerable body of their fellow-tribesmen still remained upon the Continent, where they were still independent and unconverted up to the time of Karl the Great.

The English, on the other hand, apparently migrated in a body. There is no trace of any Englishmen in Denmark or Germany after the exodus to Britain. Their language, of which a dialect still survives in Friesland, has utterly died out in Sleswick. The English took for their share of Britain the nearest east coast. We have little record of their arrival, even in the legendary story; we merely learn that in 547, Ida "succeeded to the kingdom" of the Northumbrians, whence we may possibly conclude that the colony was already established. The English settlement extended from the Forth to Essex, and was subdivided into Bernicia, Deira, and East Anglia.

Wherever the Anglo-Saxons came, their first work was to stamp out with fire and sword every trace of the Roman civilisation. Modern investigations amongst pagan Anglo-Saxon barrows in Britain show the Low German race as pure barbarians, great at destruction, but incapable of constructive work. Professor Rolleston, who has opened several of these early heathen tombs of our Teutonic ancestors, finds in them everywhere abundant evidence of "their great aptness at destroying, and their great slowness in elaborating, material civilisation." Until the Anglo-Saxon received from the Continent the Christian religion and the Roman culture, he was a mere average Aryan barbarian, with a strong taste for war and plunder, but with small love for any of the arts of peace. Wherever else, in Gaul, Spain, or Italy, the Teutonic barbarians came in contact with the Roman civilisation, they received the religion of Christ, and the arts of the conquered people, during or before their conquest of the country. But in Britain the Teutonic invaders remained pagans long after their settlement in the island; and they utterly destroyed, in the south-eastern tract, almost every relic of the Roman rule and of the Christian faith. Hence we have here the curious fact that, during the fifth and sixth centuries, a belt of intrusive and aggressive heathendom intervenes between the Christians of the Continent and the Christian Welsh and Irish of western Britain. The Church of the Celtic Welsh was cut off for more than a hundred years from the Churches of the Roman world by a hostile and impassable barrier of heathen English, Jutes, and Saxons. Their separation produced many momentous effects on the after history both of the Welsh themselves and of their English conquerors.

1. For an account of these two main authorities see further on, Bæda in chapter xi., and the "Chronicle" in chapter xviii.

* * * * *

CHAPTER IV.

THE COLONISATION OF THE COAST.

Though the myths which surround the arrival of the English in Britain have little historical value, they are yet interesting for the light which they throw incidentally upon the habits and modes of thought of the colonists. They have one character in common with all other legends, that they grow fuller and more circumstantial the further they proceed from the original time. Bæda, who wrote about A.D. 700, gives them in a very meagre form: the English Chronicle, compiled at the court of Ælfred, about A.D. 900, adds several important traditional particulars: while with the romantic Geoffrey of Monmouth, A.D. 1152, they assume the character of full and circumstantial tales. The less men knew about the conquest, the more they had to tell about it.

Among the most sacred animals of the Aryan race was the horse. Even in the Indian epics, the sacrifice of a horse was the highest rite of the primitive religion. Tacitus tells us that the Germans kept sacred white horses at the public expense, in the groves and woods of the gods: and that from their neighings and snortings, auguries were taken. Amongst the people of the northern marshlands, the white horse seems to have been held in especial honour, and to this day a white horse rampant forms the cognisance of Hanover and Brunswick. The English settlers brought this, their national emblem, with them to Britain, and cut its figure on the chalk downs as they advanced westward, to mark the progress of their conquest. The white horses on the Berkshire and Wiltshire hills still bear witness to their settlement. A white horse is even now the symbol of Kent. Hence it is not surprising to learn that in the legendary story of the first colonisation, the Jutish leaders who led the earliest Teutonic host into Thanet should bear the names of Hengest and Horsa, the stallion and the mare. They came in three keels—a ridiculously inadequate number, considering their size and the necessities of a conquering army: and they settled in 449 (for the legends are always most precise where they are least historical) in the Isle of Thanet. "A multitude of whelps," says the Welsh monk Gildas, "came forth from the lair of the barbaric lioness, in three cyuls, as they call them." Vortigern, King of the Welsh, had invited them to come to his aid against the Picts of North Britain and the Scots of Ireland, who were making piratical incursions into the deserted province, left unprotected through the heavy levies made by the departing Romans. The Jutes attacked and conquered the Gaels, but then turned against their Welsh allies.

In 455, the Jutes advanced from Thanet to conquer the whole of Kent, "and Hengest and Horsa fought with Vortigern the king," says the English Chronicle, "at the place that is cleped Æglesthrep; and there men slew Horsa his brother, and after that Hengest came to rule, and Æsc his son." One year later, Hengest and Æsc fought once more with the Welsh at Crayford, "and offslew 4,000 men; and the Britons then forsook Kent-land, and fled with mickle awe to London-bury." In this account we may see a dim recollection of the settlement of the two petty Jutish kingdoms in Kent, with their respective capitals at Canterbury and Rochester, whose separate dioceses still point back to the two original principalities. It may be worth while to note, too, that the name Æsc means the ash-tree; and that this tree was as sacred among plants as the horse was among animals.

Nevertheless, a kernel of truth doubtless lingers in the traditional story. Thanet was afterwards one of the first landing-places of the Danes: and its isolated position—for a broad belt of sea then separated the island from the Kentish main—would make it a natural post to be assigned by the Welsh to their doubtful piratical allies. The inlet was guarded by the great Roman fortress of Rhutupiæ: and after the fall of that important stronghold, the English may probably have occupied the principality of East Kent, with its capital of Canterbury. The walls of Rochester may have held out longer: and the West Kentish kingdom may well have been founded by two successful battles at the passage of the Medway and the Cray.

The legend as to the settlement of Sussex is of much the same sort. In 477, Ælle the Saxon came to Britain also with the suspiciously symmetrical number of three ships. With him came his three sons, Kymen, Wlencing, and Cissa. These names are obviously invented to account for those of three important places in the South-Saxon chieftainship. The host landed at Kymenes ora, probably Keynor, in the Bill of Selsey, then, as its title imports, a separate island girt round by the tidal sea: their capital and, in days after the Norman conquest, their cathedral was at Cissan-ceaster, the Roman Regnum, now Chichester: while the third name survives in the modern village of Lancing, near Shoreham. The Saxons at once fought the natives "and offslew many Welsh, and drove some in flight into the wood that is named Andredes-leag," now the Weald of Kent and Sussex. A little colony thus occupied the western half of the modern county: but the eastern portion still remained in the hands of the Welsh. For awhile the great Roman fortress of Anderida (now Pevensey) held out against the invaders; until in 491 "Ælle and Cissa beset Anderida, and offslew all that were therein; nor was there after even one Briton left alive." All Sussex became a single Saxon kingdom, ringed round by the great forest of the Weald. Here again the obviously unhistorical character of the main facts throws the utmost doubt upon the nature of the details. Yet, in this case too, the central idea itself is likely enough,—that the South Saxons first occupied the solitary coast islet of Selsey; then conquered the fortress of Regnum and the western shore as far as Eastbourne; and finally captured Anderida and the eastern half of the county up to the line of the Romney marshes.

Even more improbable is the story of the Saxon settlement on the more distant portion of the south coast. In 495 "came twain aldermen to Britain, Cerdic and Cynric his son, with five ships, at that place that is cleped Cerdices ora, and fought that ilk day with the Welsh." Clearly, the name of Cerdic may be invented solely to account for the name of the place: since we see by the sequel that the English freely imagined such personages as pegs on which to hang their mythical history.[1] For, six years later, one Port landed at Portsmouth with two ships, and there slew a Welsh nobleman. But we know positively that the name of Portsmouth comes from the Latin *Portus*; and therefore Port must have been simply invented to explain the unknown derivation. Still more flagrant is the case of Wihtgar, who conquered the Isle of Wight, and was buried at Wihtgarasbyrig, or Carisbrooke. For the origin of that name is really quite different: the Wiht-ware or Wiht-gare are the men of Wight, just as the Cant-ware are the men of Kent: and Wiht-gara-byrig is the Wight-men's-bury, just as Cant-wara-byrig or Canterbury is the Kent-men's-bury. Moreover, a double story is told in the Chronicle as to the original colonisation of Wessex; the first attributing the conquest to Cerdic and Cynric, and the second to Stuf and Wihtgar.

The only other existing legend refers to the great English kingdom of Northumbria: and about it the English Chronicle, which is mainly West Saxon in origin, merely tells us in dry terms under the year 547, "Here Ida came to rule." There are no details, even of the meagre kind, vouchsafed in the south; no account of the conquest of the great Roman town of York, or of the resistance offered by the powerful Brigantian tribes. But a fragment of some old Northumbrian tradition, embedded in the later and spurious Welsh compilation which bears the name of Nennius, tells us a not improbable tale—that the first settlement on the coast of the Lothians was made as early as the conquest of Kent, by Jutes of the same stock as those who colonised Thanet. A hundred years later, the Welsh poems seem to say, Ida "the flame-bearer," fought his way down from a petty principality on the Forth, and occupied the whole Northumbrian coast, in spite of the stubborn guerilla warfare of the despairing provincials. Still less do we learn about the beginnings of Mercia, the powerful English kingdom which occupied the midlands; or about the first colonisation of East Anglia. In short, the legends of the settlement, unhistorical and meagre as they are, refer only to the Jutish and Saxon conquests in the south, and tell us nothing at all about the origin of the main English kingdoms in the north. It is important to bear in mind this fact, because the current conceptions as to the spread of the Anglo-Saxon race and the extermination of the native Welsh are largely based upon the very limited accounts of the conquest of Kent and Sussex, and the mournful dirges of the Welsh monks or bards.

It seems improbable, however, that the north-eastern coast of Britain, naturally exposed above every other part to the ravages of northern pirates, and in later days the head-quarters of the Danish intruders in our island, should so long have remained free from English incursions. If the Teutonic settlers really first established themselves here a century later than their conquest of Kent, we can only account for it by the supposition that York and the Brigantes, the old metropolis of the provinces, held out far more stubbornly and successfully than Rochester and Anderida, with their very servile Romanised population. But even the words of the Chronicle do not necessarily imply that Ida was the first king of the Northumbrians, or that the settlement of the country took place in his days.[2] And if they did, we need not feel bound to accept their testimony, considering that the earliest date we can assign for the composition of the chronicle is the reign of Ælfred: while Bæda, the earlier native Northumbrian historian, throws no light at all upon the question. Hence it seems probable that Nennius preserves a truthful tradition, and that the English settled in the region between the Forth and the Tyne, at least as early as the Jutes settled in Kent or the Saxons along the South Coast, from Pevensey Bay to Southampton Water.

If, then, we leave out of consideration the etymological myths and numerical absurdities of the English or Welsh legends, and look only at the facts disclosed to us by the subsequent condition of the country, we shall find that the early Anglo-Saxon settlements took place somewhat after this wise. In the extreme north, the English apparently did not care to settle in the rugged mountain country between Aberdeen and Edinburgh, inhabited by the free and warlike Picts. But from the Firth of Forth to the borders of Essex, a succession of colonies, belonging to the restricted English tribe, occupied the whole provincial coast, burning, plundering, and massacring in many places as they went. First and northernmost of all came the people whom we know by their Latinised title of Bernicians, and who descended upon the rocky braes between Forth and Tyne. These are the English of Ida's kingdom, the modern Lothians and Northumberland. Their chief town was at Bebbanburh, now Bamborough, which Ida "timbered, and betyned it with a hedge." Next in geographical order stood the people of Deira, or Yorkshire, who occupied the rich agricultural valley of the Ouse, the fertile alluvial tract of Holderness, and the bleak coast-line from Tyne to Humber. Whether they conquered the Roman capital of York, or whether it made terms with the invaders, we do not know; but it is not mentioned as the chief town of the English kings before the days of Eadwine, under whom the two Northumbrian chieftainships were united into a single kingdom. However, as Eadwine assumed some of the imperial Roman trappings, it seems not unlikely that a portion at least of the Romanised population survived the conquest. The two principalities probably spread back politically in most places as far as the watershed which separates the basins of the German Ocean and the Irish Sea; but the English population seems to have lived mainly along the coast or in the fertile valley of the Ouse and its tributaries; for Elmet and Loidis, two Welsh principalities, long held out in the Leeds district, and the people of the dales and the inland parts, as we shall see reason hereafter to conclude, even now show evident marks of Celtic descent. Together the two chieftainships were generally known by the name of Northumberland, now confined to their central portion; but it must never be forgotten that the Lothians, which at present form part of modern Scotland, were originally a portion of this early English kingdom, and are still, perhaps, more purely English in blood and speech than any other district in our island.

From Humber to the Wash was occupied by a second English colony, the men of Lincolnshire, divided into three minor tribes, one of which, the Gainas, has left its name to Gainsborough. Here, again, we hear nothing of the conquest, nor of the means by which the powerful Roman colony of Lincoln fell into the hands of the English. But the town still retains its Roman name, and in part its Roman walls; so that we may conclude the native population was not entirely exterminated.

East Anglia, as its name imports, was likewise colonised by an English horde, divided, like the men of Kent, into two minor bodies, the North Folk and the South Folk, whose names survive in the modern counties of Norfolk and Suffolk. But in East Anglia, as in Yorkshire, we shall see reason hereafter to conclude that the lower orders of Welsh were largely spared, and that their descendants still form in part the labouring classes of the two counties. Here, too, the English settlers probably clustered thickest along the coast, like the Danes in later days; and the great swampy expanse of the Fens, then a mere waste of marshland tenanted by beavers and wild fowl, formed the inland boundary or mark of their almost insular kingdom.

The southern half of the coast was peopled by Englishmen of the Saxon and Jutish tribes. First came the country of the East Saxons, or Essex, the flat land stretching from the borders of East Anglia to the estuary of the Thames. This had been one of the most thickly-populated Roman regions, containing the important stations of Camalodunum, London, and Verulam. But we know nothing, even by report, of its conquest. Beyond it, and separated by the fenland of the Lea, lay the outlying little principality of Middlesex. The upper reaches of the Thames were still in the hands of the Welsh natives, for the great merchant city of London blocked the way for the pirates to the head-waters of the river.

On the south side of the estuary lay the Jutish principalities of East and West Kent, including the strong Roman posts of Rhutupiæ, Dover, Rochester, and Canterbury. The great forest of the Weald and the Romney Marshes separated them from Sussex; and the insular positions of Thanet and Sheppey had always special attractions for the northern pirates.

Beyond the marshes, again, the strip of southern shore, between the downs and the sea, as far as Hayling Island, fell into the hands of the South Saxons, whose boundary to the east was formed by Romney Marsh, and to the west by the flats near Chichester, where the forest runs down to the tidal swamp by the sea. The district north of the Weald, now known as Surrey, was also peopled by Saxon freebooters, at a later date, though doubtless far more sparsely.

Finally, along the wooded coast from Portsmouth to Poole Harbour, the Gewissas, afterwards known as the West Saxons, established their power. The Isle of Wight and the region about Southampton Water, however, were occupied by the Meonwaras, a small intrusive colony of Jutes. Up the rich valley overlooked by the great Roman city of Winchester (Venta Belgarum), the West Saxons made their way, not without severe opposition, as their own legends and traditions tell us; and in Winchester they fixed their capital for awhile. The long chain of chalk downs behind the city formed their weak northern mark or boundary, while to the west they seem always to have carried on a desultory warfare with the yet unsubdued Welsh, commanded by their great leader Ambrosius, who has left his name to Ambres-byrig, or Amesbury.

We must not, however, suppose that each of these colonies had from the first a united existence as a political community. We know that even the eight or ten kingdoms into which England was divided at the dawn of the historical period were each themselves produced by the consolidation of several still smaller chieftainships. Even in the two petty Kentish kingdoms there were under-kings, who had once been independent. Wight was a distinct kingdom till the reign of Ceadwalla in Wessex. The later province of Mercia was composed of minor divisions, known as the

Hwiccas, the Middle English, the West Hecan, and so forth. Henry of Huntingdon, a historian of the twelfth century, who had access, however, to several valuable and original sources of information now lost, tells us that many chieftains came from Germany, occupied Mercia and East Anglia, and often fought with one another for the supremacy. In fact, the petty kingdoms of the eighth century were themselves the result of a consolidation of many forgotten principalities founded by the first conquerors.

Thus the earliest England with which we are historically acquainted consisted of a mere long strip or borderland of Teutonic coast, divided into tiny chieftainships, and girding round half of the eastern and southern shores of a still Celtic Britain. Its area was discontinuous, and its inland boundaries towards the back country were vaguely defined. As Massachusetts and Connecticut stood off from Virginia and Georgia— as New South Wales and Victoria stand off from South Australia and Queensland—so Northumbria stood off from East Anglia, and Kent from Sussex. Each colony represented a little English nucleus along the coast or up the mouths of the greater rivers, such as the Thames and Humber, where the pirates could easily drive in their light craft. From such a nucleus, perched at first on some steep promontory like Bamborough, some separate island like Thanet, Wight, and Selsey, or some long spit of land like Holderness and Hurst Castle, the barbarians could extend their dominions on every side, till they reached some natural line of demarcation in the direction of their nearest Teutonic neighbours, which formed their necessary mark. Inland they spread as far as they could conquer; but coastwise the rivers and fens were their limits against one another. Thus this oldest insular England is marked off into at least eight separate colonies by the Forth, the Tyne, the Humber, the Wash, the Harwich Marshes, the Thames, the Weald Forest, and the Chichester tidal swamp region. As to how the pirates settled down along this wide stretch of coast, we know practically nothing; of their westward advance we know a little, and as time proceeds, that knowledge becomes more and more.

1. Cerdic is apparently a British rather than an English name, since Bæda mentions a certain "Cerdic, rex Brettonum." This may have been a Caradoc. Perhaps the first element in the names Cerdices ora, Cerdices ford, &c., was older than the English conquest. The legends are invariably connected with local names.
2. A remarkable passage in the Third Continuator of Florence mentions Hyring as the first king of Bernicia, followed by Woden and five other mythical personages, before Ida. Clearly, this is mere unhistorical guesswork on the part of the monk of Bury; but it may enclose a genuine tradition so far as Hyring is concerned.

* * * * *

CHAPTER V.

THE ENGLISH IN THEIR NEW HOMES.

If any trust at all can be placed in the legends, a lull in the conquest followed the first settlement, and for some fifty years the English—or at least the West Saxons—were engaged in consolidating their own dominions, without making any further attack upon those of the Welsh. It may be well, therefore, to enquire what changes of manners had come over them in consequence of their change of place from the shores of the Baltic and the North Sea to those of the Channel and the German Ocean.

As a whole, English society remained much the same in Britain as it had been in Sleswick and North Holland. The English came over in a body, with their women and children, their flocks and herds, their goods and chattels. The peculiar breed of cattle which they brought with them may still be distinguished in their remains from the earlier Celtic short-horn associated with Roman ruins and pre-historic barrows. They came as settlers, not as mere marauders; and they remained banded together in their original tribes and families after they had occupied the soil of Britain.

From the moment of their landing in Britain the savage corsairs of the Sleswick flats seem wholly to have laid aside their seafaring habits. They built no more ships, apparently; for many years after Bishop Wilfrith had to teach the South Saxons how to catch sea-fish; while during the early Danish incursions we hear distinctly that the English had no vessels; nor is there much incidental mention of shipping between the age of the settlement and that of Ælfred. The new-comers took up their abode at once on the richest parts of Roman Britain, and came into full enjoyment of orchards which they had not planted and fields which they had not sown. The state of cultivation in which they found the vale of York and the Kentish glens must have been widely different from that to which they were accustomed in their old heath-clad home. Accordingly, they settled down at once into farmers and landowners on a far larger scale than of yore; and they were not anxious to move away from the rich lands which they had so easily acquired. From being sailors and graziers they took to be agriculturists and landmen. In the towns, indeed, they did not settle; and most of these continued to bear their old Roman or Celtic titles. A few may have been destroyed, especially in the first onset, like Anderida, and, at a later date, Chester; but the greater number seem to have been still scantily inhabited, under English protection, by a mixed urban population, mainly Celtic in blood, and known by the name of Loegrians. It was in the country, however, that the English conquerers took up their abode. They were tillers of the soil, not merchants or skippers, and it was long before they acquired a taste for urban life. The whole eastern half of England is filled with villages bearing the characteristic English clan names, and marking each the home of a distinct family of early settlers. As soon as the new-comers had burnt the villa of the old Roman proprietor, and killed, driven out, or enslaved his abandoned serfs, they took the land to themselves and divided it out on their national system. Hence the whole government and social organisation of England is purely Teutonic, and the country even lost its old name of Britain for its new one of England.

In England, as of old in Sleswick, the village community formed the unit of English society. Each such township was still bounded by its mark of forest, mere, or fen, which divided it from its nearest neighbours. In each lived a single clan, supposed to be of kindred blood and bearing a common name. The marksmen and their serfs, the latter being conquered Welshmen, cultivated the soil under cereals for bread, and also for an unnecessarily large supply of beer, as we learn at a later date from numerous charters. Cattle and horses grazed in the pastures, while large herds of pigs were kept in the forest which formed the mark. Thus the early English settled down at once from a nation of pirates into one of agriculturists. Here and there, among the woods and fens which still covered a large part of the country, their little separate communities rose in small fenced clearings or on low islets, now joined by drainage to the mainland; while in the wider valleys, tilled in Roman times, the wealthier chieftains formed their settlements and allotted lands to their Welsh tributaries. Many family names appear in different parts of England, for a reason which will hereafter be explained. Thus we find the Bassingas at Bassingbourn, in Cambridgeshire; at Bassingfield, in Notts; at Bassingham and Bassingthorpe, in Lincolnshire; and at Bassington, in Northumberland. The Billings have left their stamp at Billing, in Northampton; Billingford, in Norfolk; Billingham, in Durham; Billingley, in Yorkshire; Billinghurst, in Sussex; and five other places in various other counties. Birmingham, Nottingham, Wellington, Faringdon, Warrington, and Wallingford are well-known names formed on the same analogy. How thickly these clan settlements lie scattered over Teutonic England may be judged from the number which occur in the London district alone—Kensington, Paddington, Notting-hill, Billingsgate, Islington, Newington, Kennington, Wapping, and Teddington. There are altogether 1,400 names of this type in England. Their value as a test of Teutonic colonisation is shown by the fact that while 48 occur in Northumberland, 127 in Yorkshire, 76 in Lincolnshire, 153 in Norfolk and Suffolk, 48 in Essex, 60 in Kent, and 86 in Sussex and Surrey, only 2 are found in Cornwall, 6 in Cumberland, 24 in Devon, 13 in Worcester, 2 in Westmoreland, and none in Monmouth. Speaking generally, these clan names are thickest along the original English coast, from Forth to Portland; they decrease rapidly as we move inland; and they die away altogether as we approach the purely Celtic west.

The English families, however, probably tilled the soil by the aid of Welsh slaves; indeed, in Anglo-Saxon, the word serf and Welshman are used almost interchangeably as equivalent synonyms. But though many Welshmen were doubtless spared from the very first, nothing is more certain than the fact that they became thoroughly Anglicized. A few new words from Welsh or Latin were introduced into the English tongue, but they were far too few sensibly to affect its vocabulary. The language was and still is essentially Low German; and though it now contains numerous words of Latin or French origin, it does not and never did contain any but the very smallest Celtic element. The slight number of additions made from the Welsh consisted chiefly of words connected with the higher Roman civilisation—such as wall, street, and chester—or the new methods of agriculture which the Teuton learnt from his more civilised serfs. The Celt has always shown a great tendency to cast aside his native language in Gaul, in Spain, and in Ireland; and the isolation of the English townships must have had the effect of greatly accelerating the process. Within a few generations the Celtic slave had forgotten his tongue, his origin, and his religion, and had developed into a pagan English serf. Whatever else the Teutonic conquest did, it turned every man within the English pale into a thorough Englishman.

But the removal to Britain effected one immense change. "War begat the king." In Sleswick the English had lived within their little marks as free and independent communities. In Britain all the clans of each colony gradually came under the military command of a king. The ealdormen who led the various marauding bands assumed royal power in the new country. Such a change was indeed inevitable. For not only had the English to win the new England, but they had also to keep it and extend it. During four hundred years a constant smouldering warfare was carried on between the foreigners and the native Welsh on their western frontier. Thus the townships of each colony entered into a closer union with one another for military purposes, and so arose the separate chieftainships or petty kingdoms of early England. But the king's power was originally very small. He was merely the semi-hereditary general and representative of the people, of royal stock, but elected by the free suffrages of the freemen. Only as the kingdoms coalesced, and as the power of meeting became consequently less, did the king acquire his greater prerogatives. From the first, however, he seems to have possessed the right of granting public lands, with the consent of the freemen, to particular individuals; and such book-land, as the early English called it, after the introduction of Roman writing, became the origin of our system of private property in land.

Every township had its moot or assembly of freemen, which met around the sacred oak, or on some holy hill, or beside the great stone monument of some forgotten Celtic chieftain. Every hundred also had its moot, and many of these still survive in their original form to the present day, being held in the open air, near some sacred site or conspicuous landmark. And the colony as a whole had also its moot, at which all freemen might attend, and which settled the general affairs of the kingdom. At these last-named moots the kings were elected; and though the selection was practically confined to men of royal kin, the king nevertheless represented the free choice of the tribe. Before the conversion to Christianity, the royal families all traced their origin to Woden. Thus the pedigree of Ida, King of Northumbria, runs as follows:—"Ida was Eopping, Eoppa was Esing, Esa was Inguing, Ingui Angenwiting, Angenwit Alocing, Aloc Benocing, Benoc Branding, Brand Baldæging, Bældæg Wodening." But in later Christian times the chroniclers felt the necessity of reconciling these heathen genealogies with the Scriptural account in Genesis; so they affiliated Woden himself upon the Hebrew patriarchs. Thus the pedigree of the West Saxon kings, inserted in the Chronicle under the year 855, after conveying back the genealogy of Æthelwulf to Woden, continues to say, "Woden was Frealafing, Frealaf Finning," and so on till it reaches "Sceafing, *id est filius Noe*; he was born in Noe's Ark. Lamech, Mathusalem, Enoc, Jared, Malalehel, Camon, Enos, Seth, Adam, *primus homo et pater noster*."

The Anglo-Saxons, when they settled in Eastern and Southern Britain, were a horde of barbarous heathen pirates. They massacred or enslaved the civilised or half-civilised Celtic inhabitants with savage ruthlessness. They burnt or destroyed the monuments of Roman occupation. They let the roads and cities fall into utter disrepair. They stamped out Christianity with fire and sword from end to end of their new domain. They occupied a civilised and Christian land, and they restored it to its primitive barbarism. Nor was there any improvement until Christian teachers from Rome and Scotland once more introduced the forgotten culture which the English pirates had utterly destroyed. As Gildas phrases it, with true Celtic eloquence, the red tongue of flame licked up the whole land from end to end, till it slaked its horrid thirst in the western ocean. For 150 years the whole of English Britain, save, perhaps, Kent and London, was cut off from all intercourse with Christendom and the Roman world. The country consisted of several petty chieftainships, at constant feud with their Teutonic neighbours, and perpetually waging a border war with Welsh, Picts, and Scots. Within each colony, much of the land remained untilled, while the clan settlements appeared like little islands of cultivation in the midst of forest, waste, and common. The villages were mere groups of wooden homesteads, with barns and cattle-sheds, surrounded by rough stockades, and destitute of roads or communications. Even the palace of the king was a long wooden hall with numerous outhouses; for the English built no stone houses, and burnt down those of their Roman predecessors. Trade seems to have been confined to the south coast, and few manufactured articles of any sort were in use. The English degraded their Celtic serfs to their own barbaric level; and the very memory of Roman civilization almost died out of the land for a hundred and fifty years.

* * * * *

CHAPTER VI.

THE CONQUEST OF THE INTERIOR.

From the little strip of eastern and southern coast on which they first settled, the English advanced slowly into the interior by the valleys of the great rivers, and finally swarmed across the central dividing ridge into the basins of the Severn and the Irish Sea. Up the open river mouths they could make their way in their shallow-bottomed boats, as the Scandinavian pirates did three centuries later; and when they reached the head of navigation in each stream for the small draught of their light vessels, they probably took to the land and settled down at once, leaving further inland expeditions to their sons and successors. For this second step in the Teutonic colonisation of Britain we have some few traditional accounts, which seem somewhat more trustworthy than those of the first settlement. Unfortunately, however, they apply for the most part only to the kingdom of Wessex, and not to the North and the Midlands, where such details would be of far greater value.

The valley of the Humber gives access to the great central basin of the Trent. Up this fruitful basin, at a somewhat later date, apparently, than the settlement of Deira and Lincolnshire, scattered bodies of English colonists, under petty leaders whose names have been forgotten, seem to have pushed their way forward through the broad lowlands towards Derby, Nottingham, and Leicester. They bore the name of Middle English. Westward, again, other settlers raised their capital at Lichfield. These formed the advanced guard of the English against the Welsh, and hence their country was generally known as the Mark, or March, a name which was afterwards latinized into the familiar form of Mercia. The absence of all tradition as to the colonisation of this important tract, the heart of England, and afterwards one of the three dominant Anglo-Saxon states, leads one to suppose that the process was probably very gradual, and the change came about so slowly as to have left but little trace on the popular memory. At any rate, it is certain that the central ridge long formed the division between the two races; and that the Welsh at this period still occupied the whole western watershed, except in the lower portion of the Severn valley.

The Welland, the Nene, and the Great Ouse, flowing through the centre of the Fen Country, then a vast morass, studded with low and marshy islands, gave access to the districts about Peterborough, Stamford, and Cambridge. Here, too, a body of unknown settlers, the Gyrwas, seem about the same time to have planted their colonies. At a later date they coalesced with the Mercians. However, the comparative scarcity of villages bearing the English clan names throughout all these regions suggests the probability that Mercia, Middle England, and the Fen Country were not by any means so densely colonised as the coast districts; and independent Welsh communities long held out among the isolated dry tracts of the fens as robbers and outlaws.

In the south, the advance of the West Saxons had been checked in 520, according to the legend, by the prowess of Arthur, king of the Devonshire Welsh. As Mr. Guest acutely notes, some special cause must have been at work to make the Britons resist here so desperately as to maintain for half a century a weak frontier within little more than twenty miles of Winchester, the West Saxon capital. He suggests that the great choir of Ambrosius at Amesbury was probably the chief Christian monastery of Britain, and that the Welshman may here have been fighting for all that was most sacred to him on earth. Moreover, just behind stood the mysterious national monument of Stonehenge, the honoured tomb of some Celtic or still earlier aboriginal chief. But in 552, the English Chronicle tells us,

Cynric, the West Saxon king, crossed the downs behind Winchester, and descended upon the dale at Salisbury. The Roman town occupied the square hill-fort of Old Sarum, and there Cynric put the Welsh to flight and took the stronghold by storm.

The road was thus opened in the rear to the upper waters of the Thames (impassable before because of the Roman population of London), as well as towards the valley of the Bath Avon. Four years later Cynric and his son Ceawlin once more advanced as far as Barbury hill-fort, probably on a mere plundering raid. But in 571 Cuthwulf, brother of Ceawlin, again marched northward, and "fought against the Welsh at Bedford, and took four towns, Lenbury (or Leighton Buzzard), Aylesbury, Bensington (near Dorchester in Oxfordshire), and Ensham." Thus the West Saxons overran the whole upper valley of the Thames from Berkshire to above Oxford, and formed a junction with the Middle Saxons to the north of London; while eastward they spread as far as the northern boundaries of Essex. In 577 the same intruders made a still more important move. Crossing the central watershed of England, near Chippenham, they descended upon the broken valley of the Bath Avon, and found themselves the first Englishmen who reached any of the basins which point westward towards the Atlantic seaboard. At a doubtful place named Deorham (probably Dyrham near Bath), "Cuthwine and Ceawlin fought against the Welsh, and slew three kings, Conmail, and Condidan, and Farinmail, and took three towns from them, Gloucester, and Cirencester, and Bath." Thus the three great Roman cities of the lower Severn valley fell into the hands of the West Saxons, and the English for the first time stood face to face with the western sea. Though the story of these conquests is of course recorded from mere tradition at a much later date, it still has a ring of truth, or at least of probability, about it, which is wholly wanting to the earlier legends. If we are not certain as to the facts, we can at least accept them as symbolical of the manner in which the West Saxon power wormed its way over the upper basin of the Thames, and crept gradually along the southern valley of the Severn.

The victory of Deorham has a deeper importance of its own, however, than the mere capture of the three great Roman cities in the south-west of Britain. By the conquest of Bath and Gloucester, the West Saxons cut off the Welsh of Devon, Cornwall, and Somerset from their brethren in the Midlands and in Wales. This isolation of the West Welsh, as the English thenceforth called them, largely broke the power of the native resistance. Step by step in the succeeding age the West Saxons advanced by hard fighting, but with no serious difficulty, to the Axe, to the Parret, to the Tone, to the Exe, to the Tamar, till at last the West Welsh, confined to the peninsula of Cornwall, became known merely as the Cornish men, and in the reign of Æthelstan were finally subjugated by the English, though still retaining their own language and national existence. But in all the western regions the Celtic population was certainly spared to a far greater extent than in the east; and the position of the English might rather be described as an occupation than as a settlement in the strict sense of the word.

The westward progress of the Northumbrians is later and much more historical. Theodoric, son of Ida, as we may perhaps infer from the old Welsh ballads, fought long and not always successfully with Urien of Strathclyde. But in 592, says Bæda, who lived himself but three-quarters of a century later than the event he describes, "there reigned over the kingdom of the Northumbrians a most brave and ambitious king, Æthelfrith, who, more than all other nobles of the English, wasted the race of the Britons; for no one of our kings, no one of our chieftains, has rendered more of their lands either tributary to or an integral part of the English territories, whether by subjugating or expatriating the natives." In 606 Æthelfrith rounded the Peakland, now known as Derbyshire, and marched from the upper Trent upon the Roman city of Chester. There "he made a terrible slaughter of the perfidious race." Over two thousand Welsh monks from the monastery of Bangor Iscoed were slain by the heathen invader; but Bæda explains that Æthelfrith put them to death because they prayed against him; a sentence which strongly suggests the idea that the English did not usually kill non-combatant Welshmen.

The victory of Chester divided the Welsh power in the north as that of Deorham had divided it in the south. Henceforward, the Northumbrians bore rule from sea to sea, from the mouth of the Humber to the mouths of the Mersey and the Dee. Æthelfrith even kept up a rude navy in the Irish Sea. Thus the Welsh nationality was broken up into three separate and weak divisions—Strathclyde in the north, Wales in the centre, and Damnonia, or Cornwall, in the south. Against these three fragments the English presented an unbroken and aggressive front, Northumbria standing over against Strathclyde, Mercia steadily pushing its way along the upper valley of the Severn against North Wales, and Wessex advancing in the south against South Wales and the West Welsh of Somerset, Devon, and Cornwall. Thus the conquest of the interior was practically complete. There still remained, it is true, the subjugation of the west; but the west was brought under the English over-lordship by slow degrees, and in a very different manner from the east and the south coast, or even the central belt. Cornwall finally yielded under Æthelstan; Strathclyde was gradually absorbed by the English in the south and the Scottish kingdom on the north; and the last remnant of Wales only succumbed to the intruders under the rule of the Angevin Edward I.

There were, in fact, three epochs of English extension in Britain. The first epoch was one of colonisation on the coasts and along the valleys of the eastward rivers. The second epoch was one of conquest and partial settlement in the central plateau and the westward basins. The third epoch was one of merely political subjugation in the western mountain regions. The proofs of these assertions we must examine at length in the succeeding chapter.

* * * * *

CHAPTER VII.

THE NATURE AND EXTENT OF THE ENGLISH SETTLEMENT.

It has been usual to represent the English conquest of South-eastern Britain as an absolute change of race throughout the greater part of our island. The Anglo-Saxons, it is commonly believed, came to England and the Lowlands of Scotland in overpowering numbers, and actually exterminated or drove into the rugged west the native Celts. The population of the whole country south of Forth and Clyde is supposed to be now, and to have been ever since the conquest, purely Teutonic or Scandinavian in blood, save only in Wales, Cornwall, and, perhaps, Cumberland and Galloway. But of late years this belief has met with strenuous opposition from several able scholars; and though many of our greatest historians still uphold the Teutonic theory, with certain modifications and admissions, there are, nevertheless, good reasons which may lead us to believe that a large proportion of the Celts were spared as tillers of the soil, and that Celtic blood may yet be found abundantly even in the most Teutonic portions of England.

In the first place, it must be remembered that, by common consent, only the east and south coasts and the country as far as the central dividing ridge can be accounted as to any overwhelming extent English in blood. It is admitted that the population of the Scottish Highlands, of Wales, and of Cornwall is certainly Celtic. It is also admitted that there exists a large mixed population of Celts and Teutons in Strathclyde and

Cumbria, in Lancashire, in the Severn Valley, in Devon, Somerset, and Dorset. The northern and western half of Britain is acknowledged to be mainly Celtic. Thus the question really narrows itself down to the ethnical peculiarities of the south and east.

Here, the surest evidence is that of anthropology. We know that the pure Anglo-Saxons were a round-skulled, fair-haired, light-eyed, blonde-complexioned race; and we know that wherever (if anywhere) we find unmixed Germanic races at the present day, High Dutch, Low Dutch, or Scandinavian, we always meet with some of these same personal peculiarities in almost every individual of the community. But we also know that the Celts, originally themselves a similar blonde Aryan race, mixed largely in Britain with one or more long-skulled dark-haired, black-eyed, and brown-complexioned races, generally identified with the Basques or Euskarians, and with the Ligurians. The nation which resulted from this mixture showed traces of both types, being sometimes blonde, sometimes brunette; sometimes black-haired, sometimes red-haired, and sometimes yellow-haired. Individuals of all these types are still found in the undoubtedly Celtic portions of Britain, though the dark type there unquestionably preponderates so far as numbers are concerned. It is this mixed race of fair and dark people, of Aryan Celts with non-Aryan Euskarians or Ligurians, which we usually describe as Celtic in modern Britain, by contradistinction to the later wave of Teutonic English.

Now, according to the evidence of the early historians, as interpreted by Mr. Freeman and other authors (whose arguments we shall presently examine), the English settlers in the greater part of South Britain almost entirely exterminated the Celtic population. But if this be so, how comes it that at the present day a large proportion of our people, even in the east, belong to the dark and long-skulled type? The fact is that upon this subject the historians are largely at variance with the anthropologists; and as the historical evidence is weak and inferential, while the anthropological evidence is strong and direct, there can be very little doubt which we ought to accept. Professor Huxley [Essay "On some

Fixed Points in British Ethnography,"] has shown that the melanochroic or dark type of Englishmen is identical in the shape of the skull, the anatomical peculiarities, and the colour of skin, hair, and eyes with that of the continent, which is undeniably Celtic in the wider sense—that is to say, belonging to the primitive non-Teutonic race, which spoke a Celtic language, and was composed of mixed Celtic, Iberian, and Ligurian elements. Professor Phillips points out that in Yorkshire, and especially in the plain of York, an essentially dark, short, non-Teutonic type is common; while persons of the same characteristics abound among the supposed pure Anglians of Lincolnshire. They are found in great numbers in East Anglia, and they are not rare even in Kent. In Sussex and Essex they occur less frequently, and they are also comparatively scarce in the Lothians. Dr. Beddoe, Dr. Thurnam, and other anthropologists have collected much evidence to the same effect. Hence we may conclude with great probability that large numbers of the descendants of the dark Britons still survive even on the Teutonic coast. As to the descendants of the light Britons, we cannot, of course, separate them from those of the like-complexioned English invaders. But in truth, even in the east itself, save only perhaps in Sussex and Essex, the dark and fair types have long since so largely coalesced by marriage that there are probably few or no real Teutons or real Celts individually distinguishable at all. Absolutely fair people, of the Scandinavian or true German sort, with very light hair and very pale blue eyes, are almost unknown among us; and when they do occur, they occur side by side with relations of every other shade. As a rule, our people vary infinitely in complexion and anatomical type, from the quite squat, long-headed, swarthy peasants whom we sometimes meet with in rural Yorkshire, to the tall, flaxen-haired, red-cheeked men whom we occasionally find not only in Danish Derbyshire, but even in mainly Celtic Wales and Cornwall. As to the west, Professor Huxley declares, on purely anthropological grounds, that it is probably, on the whole, more deeply Celtic than Ireland itself.

These anthropological opinions are fully borne out by those scientific archæologists who have done most in the way of exploring the tombs and other remains of the early Anglo-Saxon invaders. Professor Rolleston, who has probably examined more skulls of this period than any other investigator, sums up his consideration of those obtained from Romano-British and Anglo-Saxon interments by saying, "I should be inclined to think that wholesale massacres of the conquered Romano-Britons were rare, and that wholesale importations of Anglo-Saxon women were not much more frequent." He points out that "we have anatomical evidence for saying that two or more distinct varieties of men existed in England both previously to and during the period of the Teutonic invasion and domination." The interments show us that the races which inhabited Britain before the English conquest continued in part to inhabit it after that conquest. The dolichocephali, or long-skulled type of men, who, in part, preceded the English, "have been found abundantly in the Suffolk region of the Littus Saxonicum, where the Celt and Saxon [Englishman] are not known to have met as enemies when East Anglia became a kingdom." Thus we see that just where people of the dark type occur abundantly at the present day, skulls of the corresponding sort are met with abundantly in interments of the Anglo-Saxon period. Similarly, Mr. Akerman, after explorations in tombs, observes, "The total expulsion or extinction of the Romano-British population by the invaders will scarcely be insisted upon in this age of enquiry." Nay, even in Teutonic Kent, Jute and Briton still lie side by side in the same sepulchres. Most modern Englishmen have somewhat long rather than round skulls. The evidence of archæology supports the evidence of anthropology in favour of the belief that some, at least, of the native Britons were spared by the invading host.

On the other hand, against these unequivocal testimonies of modern research we have to set the testimony of the early historical authorities, on which the Teutonic theory mainly relies. The authorities in question are three, Gildas, Bæda, and the English Chronicle. Gildas was, or professes to be, a British monk, who wrote in the very midst of the English conquest, when the invaders were still confined, for the most part, to the south-eastern region. Objections have been raised to the authenticity of his work, a small rhetorical Latin pamphlet, entitled, "The History of the Britons;" but these objections have, perhaps, been set at rest for many minds by Dr. Guest and Mr. Green. Nevertheless, what little Gildas has to tell us is of slight historical importance. His book is a disappointing Jeremiad, couched in the florid and inflated Latin rhetoric so common during the decadence of the Roman empire, intermingled with a strong flavour of hyperbolical Celtic imagination; and it teaches us practically nothing as to the state of the conquered districts. It is wholly occupied with fierce diatribes against the Saxons, and complaints as to the weakness, wickedness, and apathy of the British chieftains. It says little that can throw any light on the question as to whether the Welsh were largely spared, though it abounds with wild and vague declamation about the extermination of the natives. Even Gildas, however, mentions that some of his countrymen, "constrained by famine, came and yielded themselves up to their enemies as slaves for ever;" while others, "committing the safeguard of their lives to mountains, crags, thick forests, and rocky isles, though with trembling hearts, remained in their fatherland." These passages certainly suggest that a Welsh remnant survived in two ways within the English pale, first as slaves, and secondly as isolated outlaws.

Bæda stands on a very different footing. His authenticity is undoubted; his language is simple and straightforward. He was born in or about the year 672, only two hundred years after the landing of the first English colonists in Thanet. Scarcely more than a century separated him from the days of Ida. The constant lingering warfare with the Welsh on the western frontier was still for him a living fact. The Celt still held half of Britain. At the date of his birth the northern Welsh still retained their independence in Strathclyde; the Welsh proper still spread to the banks of the Severn; and the West Welsh of Cornwall still owned all the peninsula south of the Bristol Channel as far eastward as the Somersetshire marshes. Beyond Forth and Clyde, the Picts yet ruled over the greater part of the Highlands, while the Scots, who have now given the name of Scotland to the whole of Britain beyond the Cheviots, were a mere intrusive Irish colony in Argyllshire and the Western Isles. He lived, in short, at the very period when Britain was still in the act of becoming England; and no historical doubts of any sort hang over the authenticity of his great work, "The Ecclesiastical History of the English people." But Bæda unfortunately knows little more about the first settlement than he could learn from Gildas, whom he quotes almost *verbatim*. He tells us, however, nothing of extermination of the Welsh. "Some," he says, "were slaughtered; some gave themselves up to undergo slavery: some retreated beyond the sea: and some, remaining in their own land, lived a miserable life in the mountains and forests." In all this, he is merely transcribing Gildas, but he saw no improbability in the words. At a later date, Æthelfrith, of Northumbria, he tells us, "rendered more of their lands either tributary to or an integral part of the English territory, whether by subjugating or expatriating[1] the natives," than any previous king. Eadwine, before his conversion, "subdued to the empire of the English the Mevanian islands," Man and Anglesey; but we know that the population of both islands is still mainly Celtic in blood and speech. These examples sufficiently show us, that even before the introduction of Christianity, the English did not always utterly destroy the Welsh inhabitants of conquered districts. And it is universally admitted that, after their conversion, they fought with the Welsh in a milder manner, sparing their lives as fellow-Christians, and permitting them to retain their lands as tributary proprietors.

The English Chronicle, our third authority, was first compiled at the court of Ælfred, four and a-half centuries after the Conquest; and so its value as original testimony is very slight. Its earlier portions are mainly condensed from Bæda; but it contains a few fragments of traditional information from some other unknown sources. These fragments, however, refer chiefly to Kent, Sussex, and the older parts of Wessex, where we have reason to believe that the Teutonic colonisation was exceptionally thorough; and they tell us nothing about Yorkshire,

Lincolnshire, and East Anglia, where we find at the present day so large a proportion of the population possessing an unmistakably Celtic physique. The Chronicle undoubtedly describes the conflict in the south as sharp and bloody; and in spite of the mythical character of the names and events, it is probable that in this respect it rightly preserves the popular memory of the conquest, and its general nature. In Kent, "the Welsh fled the English like fire;" and Hengest and Æsc, in a single battle, slew 4,000 men. In Sussex, Ælle and Cissa killed or drove out the natives in the western rapes on their first landing, and afterwards massacred every Briton at Anderida. In Wessex, in the first struggle, "Cerdic and Cynric offslew a British king whose name was Natanleod, and 5,000 men with him." And so the dismal annals of rapine and slaughter run on from year to year, with simple, unquestioning conciseness, showing us, at least, the manner in which the later English believed their forefathers had acquired the land. Moreover, these frightful details accord well enough with the vague generalities of Gildas, from which, however, they may very possibly have been manufactured. Yet even the Chronicle nowhere speaks of absolute extermination: that idea has been wholly read into its words, not directly inferred from them. A great deal has been made of the massacre at Pevensey; but we hear nothing of similar massacres at the great Roman cities—at London, at York, at Verulam, at Bath, at Cirencester, which would surely have attracted more attention than a small outlying fortress like Anderida. Even the Teutonic champions themselves admit that some, at least, of the Celts were incorporated into the English community. "The women," says Mr. Freeman, "would, doubtless, be largely spared;" while as to the men, he observes, "we may be sure that death, emigration, or personal slavery were the only alternatives which the vanquished found at the hands of our fathers." But there is a vast gulf, from the ethnological point of view, between exterminating a nation and enslaving it.[2]

In the cities, indeed, it would seem that the Britons remained in great numbers. The Welsh bards complain that the urban race of Romanised natives known as Loegrians, "became as Saxons." Mr. Kemble has shown that the English did not by any means always massacre the inhabitants of the cities. Mr. Freeman observes, "It is probable that within the [English] frontier there still were Roman towns tributary to the conquerors rather than occupied by them;" and Canon Stubbs himself remarks, that "in some of the cities there were probably elements of continuous life: London, the mart of the merchants, York, the capital of the north, and some others, have a continuous political existence." "Wherever the cities were spared," he adds, "a portion, at least, of the city population must have continued also. In the country, too, especially towards the west and the debateable border, great numbers of Britons may have survived in a servile or half-servile condition." But we must remember that in only two cases, Anderida and Chester, do we actually hear of massacres; in all the other towns, Bæda and the Chronicle tell us nothing about them. It is a significant fact that Sussex, the one kingdom in which we hear of a complete annihilation, is the very one where the Teutonic type of physique still remains the purest. But there are nowhere any traces of English clan nomenclature in any of the cities. They all retain their Celtic or Roman names. At Cambridge itself, in the heart of the true English country, the charter of the thegn's guild, a late document, mentions a special distinction of penalties for killing a Welshman, "if the slain be a ceorl, 2 ores, if he be a Welshman, one ore." "The large Romanised towns," says Professor Rolleston, "no doubt made terms with the Saxons, who abhorred city life, and would probably be content to leave the unwarlike burghers in a condition of heavily-taxed submissiveness."

Thus, even in the east it is admitted that a Celtic element probably entered into the population in three ways,—by sparing the women, by making rural slaves of the men, and by preserving some, at least, of the inhabitants of cities. The skulls of these Anglicised Welshmen are found in ancient interments; their descendants are still to be recognised by their physical type in modern England. "It is quite possible," says Mr. Freeman, "that even at the end of the sixth century there may have been within the English frontier inaccessible points where detached bodies of Welshmen still retained a precarious independence." Sir F. Palgrave has collected passages tending to show that parties of independent Welshmen held out in the Fens till a very late period; and this conclusion is admitted by Mr. Freeman to be probably correct. But more important is the general survival of scattered Britons within the English communities themselves. Traces of this we find even in Anglo-Saxon documents. The signatures to very early charters,[3] collected by Thorpe and Kemble, supply us with names some of which are assuredly not Teutonic, while others are demonstrably Celtic; and these names are borne by people occupying high positions at the court of English kings. Names of this class occur even in Kent itself; while others are borne by members of the royal family of Wessex. The local dialect of the West Riding of Yorkshire still contains many Celtic words; and the shepherds of Northumberland and the Lothians still reckon their sheep by what is known as "the rhyming score," which is really a corrupt form of the Welsh numerals from one to twenty. The laws of Northumbria mention the Welshmen who pay rent to the king. Indeed, it is clear that even in the east itself the English were from the first a body of rural colonists and landowners, holding in subjection a class of native serfs, with whom they did not intermingle, but who gradually became Anglicised, and finally coalesced with their former masters, under the stress of the Danish and Norman supremacies.

In the west, however, the English occupation took even less the form of a regular colonisation. The laws of Ine, a West Saxon king, show us that in his territories, bordering on yet unconquered British lands, the Welshman often occupied the position of a rent-paying inferior, as well as that of a slave. The so-called Nennius tells us that Elmet in Yorkshire, long an intrusive Welsh principality, was not subdued by the English till the reign of Eadwine of Northumbria; when, we learn, the Northumbrian prince "seized Elmet, and expelled Cerdic its king:" but nothing is said as to any extermination of its people. As Bæda incidentally mentions this Cerdic, "king of the Britons," Nennius may probably be trusted upon the point. As late as the beginning of the tenth century, King Ælfred in his will describes the people of Devon, Dorset, Somerset, and Wilts, as "Welsh kin." The physical appearance of the peasantry in the Severn valley, and especially in Shropshire, Worcestershire, Gloucestershire, and Herefordshire, indicates that the western parts of Mercia were equally Celtic in blood. The dialect of Lancashire contains a large Celtic infusion. Similarly, the English clan-villages decrease gradually in numbers as we move westward, till they almost disappear beyond the central dividing ridge. We learn from Domesday Book that at the date of the Norman conquest the number of serfs was greater from east to west, and largest on the Welsh border. Mr. Isaac Taylor points out that a similar argument may be derived from the area of the hundreds in various counties. The hundred was originally a body of one hundred English families (more or less), bound together by mutual pledge, and answerable for one another's conduct. In Sussex, the average number of square miles in each hundred is only twenty-three; in Kent, twenty-four; in Surrey, fifty-eight; and in Herts, seventy-nine: but in Gloucester it is ninety-seven; in Derby, one hundred and sixty-two; in Warwick, one hundred and seventy-nine; and in Lancashire, three hundred and two. These facts imply that the English population clustered thickest in the old settled east, but grew thinner and thinner towards the Welsh and Cumbrian border. Altogether, the historical evidence regarding the western slopes of England bears out Professor Huxley's dictum as to the thoroughly Celtic character of their population.

On the other hand, it is impossible to deny that Mr. Freeman and Canon Stubbs have proved their point as to the thorough Teutonisation of Southern Britain by the English invaders. Though it may be true that much Welsh blood survived in England, especially amongst the servile class, yet it is none the less true that the nation which rose upon the ruins of Roman Britain was, in form and organisation, almost purely English. The language spoken by the whole country was the same which had been spoken in Sleswick. Only a few words of Welsh origin relating to agriculture, household service, and smithcraft, were introduced by the serfs into the tongue of their masters. The dialects of the Yorkshire moors, of the Lake District, and of Dorset or Devon, spoken only by wild herdsmen in the least cultivated tracts, retained a few more evident traces of the Welsh vocabulary: but in York, in London, in Winchester, and in all the large towns, the pure Anglo-Saxon of the old England by the shores of the Baltic was alone spoken. The Celtic serfs and their descendants quickly assumed English names, talked English to one another, and soon forgot, in a few generations, that they had not always been Englishmen in blood and tongue. The whole organisation of the state, the whole social life of the people, was entirely Teutonic. "The historical civilisation," as Canon Stubbs admirably puts it, "is English and not Celtic." Though there may have been much Welsh blood left, it ran in the veins of serfs and rent-paying churls, who were of no political or social importance. These two aspects of the case should be kept carefully distinct. Had they always been separated, much of the discussion which has arisen on the subject would doubtless have been avoided; for the strongest advocates of the Teutonic theory are generally ready to allow that Celtic women, children, and slaves may have been largely spared: while the Celtic enthusiasts have thought incumbent upon them to derive English words from Welsh roots, and to trace the origin of English social institutions to Celtic models. The facts seem to indicate that while the modern English nation is largely Welsh in blood, it is wholly Teutonic in form and language. Each of us probably traces back his descent to mixed Celtic and Germanic ancestry: but while the Celts have contributed the material alone, the Teutons have contributed both the material and the form.

1. The word in the original is *exterminatis*, but of course *exterminare* then bore its etymological sense of expatriation or expulsion, if not merely of confiscation, while it certainly did not imply the idea of slaughter, connoted by the modern word.

2. In this and a few other cases, modern authorities are quoted merely to show that the essential facts of a large Welsh survival are really admitted even by those who most strongly argue in favour of the general Teutonic origin of Englishmen.
3. Kemble "On Anglo-Saxon Names." Proc. Arch. Inst., 1845.

* * * * *

CHAPTER VIII.

HEATHEN ENGLAND.

We can now picture to ourselves the general aspect of the country after the English colonies had established themselves as far west as the Somersetshire marshes, the Severn, and the Dee. The whole land was occupied by little groups of Teutonic settlers, each isolated by the mark within their own township; each tilling the ground with their own hands and those of their Welsh serfs. The townships were rudely gathered together into petty chieftainships; and these chieftainships tended gradually to aggregate into larger kingdoms, which finally merged in the three great historical divisions of Northumbria, Mercia, and Wessex; divisions that survive to our own time as the North, the Midlands, and the South. Meanwhile, most of the Roman towns were slowly depopulated and fell into disrepair, so that a "waste chester" becomes a common object in Anglo-Saxon history. Towns belong to a higher civilisation, and had little place in agricultural England. The roads were neglected for want of commerce; and trade only survived in London and along the coast of Kent, where the discovery of Frankish coins proves the existence of intercourse with the Teutonic kingdom of Neustria, which had grown up on the ruins of northern Gaul. Everywhere in Britain the Roman civilisation fell into abeyance: in improved agriculture alone did any notable relic of its existence remain. The century and a half between the conquest and the arrival of Augustine is a dreary period of unmixed barbarism and perpetual anarchy.

From time to time the older settled colonies kept sending out fresh swarms of young emigrants towards the yet unconquered west, much as the Americans and Canadians have done in our own days. Armed with their long swords and battle-axes, the new colonists went forth in family bands, under petty chieftains, to war against the Welsh; and when they had conquered themselves a district, they settled on it as lords of the soil, enslaved the survivors of their enemies, and made their leader into a king. Meanwhile, the older colonies kept up their fighting spirit by constant wars amongst themselves. Thus we read of contests between the men of Kent and the West Saxons, or between conflicting nobles in Wessex itself. Fighting, in fact, was the one business of the English freeman, and it was but slowly that he settled down into a quiet agriculturist. The influence of Christianity alone seems to have wrought the change. Before the conversion of England, all the glimpses which we get of the English freeman represent him only as a rude and turbulent warrior, with the very spirit of his kinsmen, the later wickings of the north.

An enormous amount of the country still remained overgrown with wild forest. The whole weald of Kent and Sussex, the great tract of Selwood in Wessex, the larger part of Warwickshire, the entire Peakland, the central dividing ridge between the two seas from Yorkshire to the Forth, and other wide regions elsewhere, were covered with primæval woodlands. Arden, Charnwood, Wychwood, Sherwood, and the rest, are but the relics of vast forests which once stretched over half England. The bear still lurked in the remotest thickets; packs of wolves still issued forth at night to ravage the herdsman's folds; wild boars wallowed in the fens or munched acorns under the oakwoods; deer ranged over all the heathy tracts throughout the whole island; and the wild white cattle, now confined to Chillingham Park, roamed in many spots from north to south. Hence hunting was the chief pastime of the princes and ealdormen when they were not engaged in war with one another or with the Welsh. Game, boar-flesh, and venison formed an important portion of diet throughout the whole early English period, up to the Norman conquest, and long after.

The king was the recognised head of each community, though his position was hardly more than that of leader of the nobles in war. He received an original lot in the conquered land, and remained a private possessor of estates, tilled by his Welsh slaves. He was king of the people, not of the country, and is always so described in the early monuments. Each king seems to have had a chief priest in his kingdom.

There was no distinct capital for the petty kingdoms, though a principal royal residence appears to have been usual. But the kings possessed many separate *hams* or estates in their domain, in each of which food and other material for their use were collected by their serfs. They moved about with their suite from one of these to another, consuming all that had been prepared for them in each, and then passing on to the next. The king himself made the journey in the waggon drawn by oxen, which formed his rude prerogative. Such primitive royal progresses were absolutely necessary in so disjointed a state of society, if the king was to govern at all. Only by moving about and seeing with his own eyes could he gain any information in a country where organisation was feeble and writing practically unknown: only by consuming what was grown for him on the spot where it was grown could he and his suite obtain provisions in the rude state of Anglo-Saxon communications. But such government as existed was mainly that of the local ealdormen and the village gentry.

Marriages were practically conducted by purchase, the wife being bought by the husband from her father's family. A relic of this custom perhaps still survives in the modern ceremony, when the father gives the bride in marriage to the bridegroom. Polygamy was not unknown; and it was usual for men to marry their father's widows. The wives, being part of the father's property, naturally became part of the son's heritage. Fathers probably possessed the right of selling their children into slavery; and we know that English slaves were sold at Rome, being conveyed thither by Frisian merchants.

The artizan class, such as it was, must have been attached to the houses of the chieftains, probably in a servile position. Pottery was manufactured of excellent but simple patterns. Metal work was, of course, thoroughly understood, and the Anglo-Saxon swords and knives discovered in barrows are of good construction. Every chief had also his minstrel, who sang the short and jerky Anglo-Saxon songs to the accompaniment of a harp. The dead were burnt and their ashes placed in tumuli in the north: the southern tribes buried their warriors in full military dress, and from their tombs much of the little knowledge which we possess as to their habits is derived. Thence have been taken their swords, a yard long, with ornamental hilt and double-cutting edge, often covered by runic inscriptions; their small girdle knives; their long spears; and their round, leather-faced, wooden shields. The jewellery is of gold, enriched with coloured enamel, pearl, or sliced garnet. Buckles, rings, bracelets, hairpins, necklaces, scissors, and toilet requisites were also buried with the dead. Glass drinking-cups which occur amongst the tombs, were probably imported from the continent to Kent or London; and some small trade certainly existed with the Roman world, as we learn from Bæda.

In faith the English remained true to their old Teutonic myths. Their intercourse with the Christian Welsh was not of a kind to make them embrace the religion which must have seemed to them that of slaves and enemies. Bæda tells us that the English worshipped idols, and sacrificed oxen to their gods. Many traces of their mythology are still left in our midst.

First in importance among their deities came Woden, the Odin of our Scandinavian kinsmen, whose name we still preserve in Wednesday (dies Mercurii). To him every royal family of the English traced its descent. Mr. Kemble has pointed out many high places in England which keep his name to the present day. Wanborough, in Surrey, at the heaven-water-parting of the Hog's Back, was originally Wodnesbeorh, or the hill of Woden. Wanborough, in Wiltshire, which divides the valleys of the Kennet and the Isis, has the same origin; as has also Woodnesborough in Kent.

Wonston, in Hants, was probably Woden's stone; Wambrook, Wampool, and Wansford, his brook, his pool, and his ford. All these names are redolent of that nature-worship which was so marked a portion of the Anglo-Saxon religion. Godshill, in the Isle of Wight, now crowned by a Christian church, was also probably the site of early Woden worship. The boundaries of estates, as mentioned in charters, give instances of trees, stones, and posts, used as landmarks, and dedicated to Woden, thus conferring upon them a religious sanction, like that of Hermes amongst the Greeks. Anglo-Saxon worship generally gathered around natural features; and sacred oaks, ashes, wells, hills, and rivers are among the commonest memorials of our heathen ancestors. Many of them were reconsecrated after the introduction of Christianity to saints of the church, and so have retained their character for sanctity almost to our own time.

Thunor, the same word as our modern English thunder, was practically, though not philologically, the Anglo-Saxon representative of Zeus. We are more familiar with his name in its clipped Norse form of Thor. Thursday is Thunor's day (Thunres dæg: dies Jovis) and the thunderbolt, really a polished stone axe of the aboriginal neolithic savages, was supposed to be his weapon. Thundersfield, in Surrey; Thundersley, in Essex; and Thursley, in Surrey, still preserve the memory of his sacred sites. Thurleigh, in Bedford; Thurlow, in Essex; Thursley, in Cumberland; Thursfield, in Staffordshire; and Thursford, in Norfolk, are more probably due to later Danish influence, and commemorate namesakes of the Norse Thor rather than the English Thunor.

Tiw, the philological equivalent of Zeus, answered rather in character to Ares, and had for his day Tuesday (dies Martis). Tiw's mere and Tiw's thorn occur in charters, and a few places still retain his name. Frea gives his title to Friday (dies Veneris), and Sætere to Saturday (dies Saturni). But the Anglo-Saxon worship really paid more attention to certain deified heroes,—Bældæg, Geat, and Sceaf; and to certain personified abstractions,—Wig (war), Death, and Sige (victory), than to these minor gods. And, as often happens in Polytheistic religions, there is reason to believe that the popular creed had much less reference to the gods at all than to many inferior spirits of a naturalistic sort. For the early English farmer, the world around was full of spiritual beings, half divine, half devilish. Fiends and monsters peopled the fens, and tales of their doings terrified his childhood. Spirits of flood and fell swamped his boat or misled him at night. Water nicors haunted the streams; fairies danced on the green rings of the pasture; dwarfs lived in the barrows of Celtic or neolithic chieftains, and wrought strange weapons underground. The mark, the forest, the hills, were all full for the early Englishman of mysterious and often hostile beings. At length the Weirds or Fates swept him away. Beneath the earth itself, Hel, mistress of the cold and joyless world of shades, at last received him; unless, indeed, by dying a warrior's death, he was admitted to the happy realms of Wælheal. As a whole, the Anglo-Saxon heathendom was a religion of terrorism. Evil spirits surrounded men on every side, dwelt in all solitary places, and stalked over the land by night. Ghosts dwelt in the forest; elves haunted the rude stone circles of elder days. The woodland, still really tenanted by deer, wolves, and wild boars, was also filled by popular imagination with demons and imps. Charms, spells, and incantations formed the most real and living part of the national faith; and many of these survived into Christian times as witchcraft. Some of them, and of the early myths, even continue to be repeated in the folk-lore of the present day. Such are the legends of the Wild Huntsman and of Wayland Smith. Indeed, heathendom had a strong hold over the common English mind long after the public adoption of Christianity; and heathen sacrifices continued to be offered in secret as late as the thirteenth century. Our poetry and our ordinary language is tinged with heathen ideas even in modern times.

Still more interesting, however, are those relics of yet earlier social states, which we find amongst the Anglo-Saxons themselves. The production of fire by rubbing together two sticks is a common practice amongst all savages; and it has acquired a sacred significance which causes it to live on into more civilised stages. Once a year the needfire was so lighted, and all the hearths of the village were rekindled from the blaze thus obtained. Cattle were "passed through the fire" to preserve them from the attacks of fiends; and perhaps even children were sometimes treated in the same manner. The ceremony, originally adopted, perhaps, by the English from their Celtic serfs, still lingers in remote parts of the country, as the lighting of fires on St. John's Eve. Tattooing the face was practised by the noble classes. It seems probable that the early English sacrificed human victims, as the Germans certainly did to Wuotan (the High Dutch Woden); and we know that the practice of suttee existed, and that widows slew themselves on the death of their husbands, in order to accompany them to the other world. Even more curious are the vestiges of Totemism, or primitive animal worship, common to all branches of the Aryan race, as well as to the North American Indians, the Australian black fellows, and many other savages. Totemism consists in the belief that each family is literally descended from a particular plant or animal, whose name it bears; and members of the family generally refuse to pluck the plant or kill the animal after which they are named. Of these beliefs we find apparently several traces in Anglo-Saxon life. The genealogies of the kings include such names as those of the horse, the mare, the ash, and the whale. In the very early Anglo-Saxon poem of Beowulf, two of the characters bear the names of Wulf and Eofer (boar). The wolf and the raven were sacred animals, and have left their memory in many places, as well as in such personal titles as Æthelwulf, the noble wolf. The boar was also greatly reverenced; its head was used as an amulet, or as a crest for helmets, and oaths were taken upon it till late in the middle ages. Our own boar's head at Christmas is a relic of the old belief. The sanctity of the horse and the ash has been already mentioned. Now many of the Anglo-Saxon clans bore names implying their descent from such plants or animals. Thus a charter mentions the Æscings, or sons of the ash, in Surrey; another refers to the Earnings, or sons of the eagle (earn); a third to the Heartings, or sons of the hart; a fourth to the Wylfings, or sons of the wolf; and a fifth to the Thornings, or sons of the thorn. The oak has left traces of his descendants at Oakington, in Cambridge: the birch, at Birchington, in Kent; the boar (Eofer) at Evringham, in Yorkshire; the hawk, at Hawkinge, in Kent; the horse, at Horsington, in Lincolnshire; the raven, at Raveningham, in Norfolk; the sun, at Sunning, in Berks; and the serpent (Wyrm), at Wormingford, Worminghall, and Wormington, in Essex, Bucks, and Gloucester, respectively. Every one of these objects is a common and well-known totem amongst savage tribes; and the inference that at some earlier period the Anglo-Saxons had been Totemists is almost irresistible.

Moreover, it is an ascertained fact that the custom of exogamy (marriage by capture outside the tribe), and of counting kindred on the female side alone, accompanies the low stage of culture with which Totemism is usually associated. We know also that this method of reckoning relationship obtained amongst certain Aryan tribes, such as the Picts. Traces of the ceremonial form of marriage by capture survived in England to a late date in the middle ages; and therefore the custom of exogamy, upon which the ceremony is based, must probably have existed amongst the English themselves at some earlier period. Even in the first historical age, a conquered king generally gave his daughter in marriage to his conqueror, as a mark of submission, which is a relic of the same custom. Now, if members of the various tribes—Jutes, English, and Saxons,—used at one time habitually to intermarry with one another, and to give their children the clan-name of the father, it would follow that persons bearing the same clan-name would appear in all the tribes. Such we find to be actually the case. The Hemings, for instance, are met with in six counties—York, Lincoln, Huntingdon, Suffolk, Northampton, and Somerset; the Mannings occur in English Norfolk and in Saxon Dorset; the Billings, and many other clans, have left their names over the whole land, from north to south and from east to west alike. It has often been assumed that these facts prove the intimate intermixture of the invading tribes; but the supposition of the former existence of exogamy, and consequent appearance of similar clan-names in all the tribes, seems far more probable than such an extreme mingling of different tribesmen over the whole conquered territory.[1] Part of the early English ceremony of marriage consisted in the bridegroom touching the head of the bride with a shoe, a relic, doubtless, of the original mode of capture, when the captor placed his foot on the neck of his prisoner or slave. After marriage, the wife's hair was cut short, which is a universal mark of slavery.

Thus we may divide the early English religion into four elements. First, the remnants of a very primitive savage faith, represented by the sanctity of animals and plants, by Totemism, by the needfire, and by the use of amulets, charms, and spells. Second, the relics of the old common Aryan nature-worship, found in the reverence paid to Thunor, or Thunder, who is a form of Zeus, and in the sacredness of hills, rivers, wells, fords, and the open air. Third, a system of Teutonic hero or ancestor-worship, typified by Woden, Bældæg, and the other great names of the genealogies, and having its origin in the belief in ghosts. Fourth, a deification of certain abstract ideas, such as War, Fate, Victory, and Death. But the average heathen Anglo-Saxon religion was merely a vast mass of superstition, a dark and gloomy terrorism, begotten of the vague dread of misfortune which barbarians naturally feel in a half-peopled land, where war and massacre are the highest business of every man's lifetime, and a violent death the ordinary way in which he meets his end.

1. I owe this ingenious explanation to a note in Mr. Andrew Lang's essays prefixed to Mr. Holland's translation of Aristotle's *Politics*. He has there also suggested the analysis of the clan names for traces of Totemism, whose results I have given above in part.

* * * * *

CHAPTER IX.

THE CONVERSION OF THE ENGLISH.

It was impossible that a country lying within sight of the orthodox Frankish kingdom, and enclosed between two Christian Churches on either side, should long remain in such a state of isolated heathendom. For to be cut off from Christendom was to be cut off from the whole social, political, intellectual, and commercial life of the civilised world. In Britain, as distinctly as in the Pacific Islands in our own day, the missionary was the pioneer of civilisation. The change which Christianity wrought in England in a few generations was almost as enormous as the change which it has wrought in Hawaii at the present time. Before the arrival of the missionary, there was no written literature, no industrial arts, no peace, no social intercourse between district and district. The church came as a teacher and civiliser, and in a few years the barbarous heathen English warrior had settled down into a toilsome agriculturist, an eager scholar, a peaceful law-giver, or an earnest priest. The change was not merely a change of religion, it was a revolution from a life of barbarism to a life of incipient culture, and slow but progressive civilisation.

So inevitable was the Christianisation of England, that even while the flood of paganism was pouring westward, the east was beginning to receive the faith of Rome from the Frankish kingdom and from Italy. It has been necessary, indeed, to anticipate a little, in order to show the story of the conquest in its true light. Ten years before the heathen Æthelfrith of Northumbria massacred the Welsh monks at Chester, Augustine had brought Christianity to the people of Kent.

In 596, Gregory the Great determined to send a mission to England. Even before that time, Kent had been in closer union with the Continent than any other part of the country. Trade went on with the kindred Saxon coast of the Frankish kingdom, and Æthelberht, the ambitious Kentish king, and over-lord of all England south of the Humber, had even married Bercta, a daughter of the Frankish king of Paris. Bercta was of course a Christian, and she brought her own Frankish chaplain, who officiated in the old Roman church of St. Martin, at Canterbury. But Gregory's mission was on a far larger scale. Augustine, prior of the monastery on the Cœlian Hill, was sent with forty monks to convert the heathen English. They landed in Thanet, in 597, with all the pomp of Roman civilisation and ecclesiastical symbolism. Gregory had rightly determined to try by ritual and show to impress the barbarian mind. Æthelberht, already predisposed to accept the Continental culture, and to assimilate his rude kingdom to the Roman model, met them in the open air at a solemn meeting; for he feared, says Bæda, to meet them within four walls, lest they should practice incantations upon him. The foreign monks advanced in procession to the king's presence, chanting their litanies, and displaying a silver cross. Æthelberht yielded almost at once. He and all his court became Christians; and the people, as is usual amongst barbarous tribes, quickly conformed to the faith of their rulers. Æthelberht gave the missionaries leave to build new churches, or to repair the old ones erected by the Welsh Christians. Augustine returned to Gaul, where he was consecrated as Archbishop of the English nation, at Arles. Kent became thenceforth a part of the great Continental system. Canterbury has ever since remained the metropolis of the English Church; and the modern archbishops trace back their succession directly to St. Augustine.

For awhile, the young Church seemed to make vigorous progress. Augustine built a monastery at Canterbury, where Æthelberht founded a new church to SS. Peter and Paul, to be a sort of Westminster Abbey for the tombs of all future Kentish kings and archbishops. He also restored an old Roman church in the city. The pope sent him sacramental vessels, altar cloths, ornaments, relics, and, above all, many books. Ten years later, Augustine enlarged his missionary field by ordaining two new bishops—Mellitus, to preach to the East Saxons, "whose metropolis," says Bæda, "is the city of London, which is the mart of many nations, resorting to it by sea and land;" and Justus to the episcopal see of West Kent, with his bishop-stool at Rochester. The East Saxons nominally accepted the faith at the bidding of their over-lord, Æthelberht; but the people of London long remained pagans at heart. On Augustine's death, however, all life seemed again to die out of the struggling mission. Laurentius, who succeeded him, found the labour too great for his weaker hands. In 613 Æthelberht died, and his son Eadbald at once apostatised, returning to the worship of Woden and the ancestral gods. The East Saxons drove out Mellitus, who, with Justus, retired to Gaul; and Archbishop Laurentius himself was minded to follow them. Then the Kentish king, admonished by a dream of the archbishop's, made submission, recalled the truant bishops, and restored Justus to Rochester. The Londoners, however, would not receive back Mellitus, "choosing rather to be under their idolatrous high-priests." Soon Laurentius died too, and Mellitus was called to take his place, and consecrated at last a church in London in the monastery of St. Peter. In 624, the third archbishop was carried off by gout, and Justus of Rochester succeeded to the primacy of the struggling church. Up to this point little had been gained, except the conversion of Kent itself, with its dependent kingdom of Essex—the two parts of England in closest union with the Continent, through the mercantile intercourse by way of London and Richborough.

Under the new primate, however, an unexpected opening occurred for the conversion of the North. The Northumbrian kings had now risen to the first place in Britain. Æthelfrith had done much to establish their supremacy; under Eadwine it rose to a height of acknowledged over-lordship. "As an earnest of this king's future conversion and translation to the kingdom of heaven," says Bæda, with pardonable Northumbrian patriotic pride, "even his temporal power was allowed to increase greatly, so that he did what no Englishman had done before—that is to say, he united under his own over-lordship all the provinces of Britain, whether inhabited by English or by Welsh." Eadwine now took in marriage Æthelburh, daughter of Æthelberht, and sister of the reigning Kentish king. Justus seized the opportunity to introduce the Church into Northumbria. He ordained one Paulinus as bishop, to accompany the Christian lady, to watch over her faith, and if possible to convert her husband and his people.

Gregory had planned his scheme with systematic completeness; he had decided that there should be two metropolitan provinces, of York and London (which he knew as the old Roman capitals of Britain), and that each should consist of twelve episcopal sees. Paulinus now went to York in furtherance of this comprehensive but abortive scheme. A miraculous escape from assassination, or what was reputed one, gave the Roman monk a hold over Eadwine's mind; but the king decided to put off his conversion till he had tried the efficacy of the new faith by a practical appeal. He went on an expedition against the treacherous king of the West Saxons, who had endeavoured to assassinate him, and determined to abide by the result. Having overthrown his enemy with great slaughter, he returned to his royal city of Coningsborough (the king's town), and put himself as a catechumen under the care of Paulinus. The pope himself was induced to interest himself in so promising a convert; and he wrote a couple of briefs to Eadwine and his queen. These letters, the originals of which were carefully preserved at Rome, are copied out in full by Bæda. No doubt, the honour of receiving such an epistle from the pontiff of the Eternal City was not without its effect upon the semi-barbaric mind of Eadwine, who seems in some respects to have inherited the old Roman traditions of Eboracum.

Still the king held back. To change his own faith was to change the faith of the whole nation, and he thought it well to consult his witan.

The old English assembly was always aristocratic in character, despite its ostensible democracy, for it consisted only of the heads of families; and as the kingdoms grew larger, their aristocratic character necessarily became more pronounced, as only the wealthier persons could be in attendance upon the king. The folk-moot had grown into the witena-gemot, or assembly of wise men. Eadwine assembled such a meeting on the banks of the Derwent—for moots were always held in the open air at some sacred spot—and there the priests and thegns declared their willingness to accept the new religion. Coifi, chief priest of the heathen gods, himself led the way, and flung a lance in derision at the temple of his own deities. To the surprise of all, the gods did not avenge the insult. Thereupon "King Æduin, with all the nobles and most of the common folk of his nation, received the faith and the font of holy regeneration, in the eleventh year of his reign, which is the year of our Lord's incarnation the six hundred and twenty-seventh, and about the hundred and eightieth after the arrival of the English in Britain. He was baptized at York on Easter-day, the first before the Ides of April (April 12), in the church of St. Peter the Apostle, which he himself had hastily built of wood, while he was being catechised and prepared for Baptism; and in the same city he gave the bishopric to his prelate and sponsor Paulinus. But after his Baptism he took care, by Paulinus's direction, to build a larger and finer church of stone, in the midst whereof his original chapel should be enclosed." To this day, York Minster, the lineal descendant of Eadwine's wooden church, remains dedicated to St. Peter; and the archbishops still sit in the bishop-stool of Paulinus. Part of Eadwine's later stone cathedral was discovered under the existing choir during the repairs rendered necessary by the incendiary Martin. As to the heathen temple, its traces still remained even in Bæda's day. "That place, formerly the abode of idols, is now pointed out not far from York to the westward, beyond the river Dornuentio, and is to-day called Godmundingaham, where the priest himself, through the inspiration of the true God, polluted and destroyed the altars which he himself had consecrated." So close did

Bæda live to these early heathen English times. From the date of St. Augustine's arrival, indeed, Bæda stands upon the surer ground of almost contemporary narrative.

Still the greater part of English Britain remained heathen. Kent, Essex, and Northumbria were converted, or at least their kings and nobles had been baptised: but East Anglia, Mercia, Sussex, Wessex, and the minor interior principalities were as yet wholly heathen. Indeed, the various Teutonic colonies seemed to have received Christianity in the exact order of their settlement: the older and more civilised first, the newer and ruder last. Paulinus, however, made another conquest for the church in Lindsey (Lincolnshire), "where the first who believed," says the Chronicle, "was a certain great man who hight Blecca, with all his clan." In the very same year with these successes, Justus died, and Honorius received the See of Canterbury from Paulinus at the old Roman city of Lincoln. So far the Roman missionaries remained the only Christian teachers in England: no English convert seems as yet to have taken holy orders.

Again, however, the church received a severe check. Mercia, the youngest and roughest principality, stood out for heathendom. The western colony was beginning to raise itself into a great power, under its fierce and strong old king Penda, who seems to have consolidated all the petty chieftainships of the Midlands into a single fairly coherent kingdom. Penda hated Northumbria, which, under Eadwine, had made itself the chief English state: and he also hated Christianity, which he knew only as a religion fit for Welsh slaves, not for English warriors. For twenty-two years, therefore, the old heathen king waged an untiring war against Christian Northumbria. In 633, he allied himself with Cadwalla, the Christian Welsh king of Gwynedd, or North Wales, in a war against Eadwine; an alliance which supplies one more proof that the gulf between Welsh and English was not so wide as it is sometimes represented to be. The Welsh and Mercian host met the Northumbrians at Heathfield (perhaps Hatfield Chase) and utterly destroyed them. Eadwine himself and his son Osfrith were slain. Penda and Cadwalla "fared thence, and undid all Northumbria." The country was once more divided into Deira and Bernicia, and two heathen rulers succeeded to the northern kingdom. Paulinus, taking Æthelburh, the widow of Eadwine, went by sea to Kent, where Honorius, whom he had himself consecrated, received him cordially, and gave him the vacant see of Rochester. There he remained till his death, and so for a time ended the Christian mission to York. Penda made the best of his victory by annexing the Southumbrians, the Middle English, and the Lindiswaras, as well as by conquering the Severn Valley from the West Saxons. Henceforth, Mercia stands forth as one of the three leading Teutonic states in Britain.

* * * * *

CHAPTER X.

ROME AND IONA.

It was not the Roman mission which finally succeeded in converting the North and the Midlands. That success was due to the Scottish and Pictish Church. At the end of the sixth century, Columba, an Irish missionary, crossed over to the solitary rock of Iona, where he established an abbey on the Irish model, and quickly evangelised the northern Picts. From Iona, some generations later, went forth the devoted missionaries who finally converted the northern half of England.

The native churches of the west, cut off from direct intercourse with the main body of Latin Christendom, had retained certain habits which were now regarded by Rome as schismatical. Chief among these were the date of celebrating Easter, and the uncanonical method of cutting the tonsure in a crescent instead of a circle. Augustine, shortly after his arrival, endeavoured to obtain unity between the two churches on these matters of discipline, to which great importance was attached as tests of submission to the Latin rule. He obtained from Æthelberht a safe-conduct through the heathen West-Saxon territories as far as what is now Worcestershire; and there, "on the borders of the Huiccii and the West-Saxons," says Bæda, "he convened to a colloquy the bishops and doctors of the nearest province of the Britons, in the place which, to the present day, is called in the English language, Augustine's Oak." Such open-air meetings by sacred trees or stones were universal in England both before and after its conversion. "He began to admonish them with a brotherly admonition to embrace with him the Catholic faith, and to undertake the common task of evangelising the pagans. For they did not observe Easter at the proper period: moreover, they did many other things contrary to the unity of the Church." But the Welsh were jealous of the intruders, and refused to abandon their old customs. Thereupon, Augustine declared that if they would not help him against the heathen, they would perish by the heathen. A few years later, after Augustine's death, this prediction was verified by Æthelfrith of Northumbria, whose massacre of the monks of Bangor has already been noticed.

It was in return for the destruction of Chester and the slaughter of the monks that Cadwalla joined the heathen Penda against his fellow Christian Eadwine. But the death of Eadwine left the throne open for the house of Æthelfrith, whose place Eadwine had taken. After a year of renewed heathendom, however, during part of which the Welsh Cadwalla reigned over Northumbria, Oswald, son of Æthelfrith, again united Deira and Bernicia under his own rule. Oswald was a Christian, but he had learnt his Christianity from the Scots, amongst whom he had spent his exile, and he favoured the introduction of Pictish and Scottish missionaries into Northumbria. The Italian monks who had accompanied Augustine were men of foreign speech and manners, representatives of an alien civilisation, and they attempted to convert whole kingdoms *en bloc* by the previous conversion of their rulers. Their method was political and systematic. But the Pictish and Irish preachers were men of more Britannic feelings, and they went to work with true missionary earnestness to convert the half Celtic people of Northumbria, man by man, in their own homes. Aidan, the apostle of the north, carried the Pictish faith into the Lothians and Northumberland. He placed his bishop-stool not far from the royal town of Bamborough, at Lindisfarne, the Holy Island of the Northumbrian coast. Other Celtic missionaries penetrated further south, even into the heathen realm of Penda and his tributary princes. Ceadda or Chad, the patron saint of Lichfield, carried Christianity to the Mercians. Diuma preached to the Middle English of Leicester with much success, Peada, their ealdorman, son of Penda, having himself already embraced the new faith. Penda had slain Oswald in a great battle at Maserfeld in 641; but the martyr only brought increased glory to the Christians: and Oswiu, who succeeded him, after an interval of anarchy, as king of Deira (for Bernicia now chose a king of its own), was also a zealous adherent of the Celtic missionaries. Thus the heterodox Church made rapid strides throughout the whole of the north.

Meanwhile, in the south the Latin missionaries, urged to activity, perhaps, by the Pictish successes, had been making fresh progress. In the very year when Oswald was chosen king by the Northumbrians, Birinus, a priest from northern Italy, went by command of the pope to the West Saxons: and after twelve months he was able to baptise their king, Cynegils, at his capital of Dorchester, on the Thames, his sponsor being Oswald of Northumbria. A year later, Felix, a Burgundian, "preached the faith of Christ to the East Anglians," who had indeed been converted by the Augustinian missionaries, but afterwards relapsed. Only Sussex and Mercia still remained heathen. But, in 655, Penda made a last attempt against Northumbria, which he had harried year after year, and was met by Oswiu at Winwidfield, near Leeds; the Christians were successful, and Penda was slain, together with thirty royal persons—petty princes of the tributary Mercian states, no doubt. His son, Peada, the Christian ealdorman of the Middle English, succeeded him, and the Mercians became Christians of the Pictish or Irish type. "Their first bishop," says Bæda, "was Diuma, who died and was buried among the Middle English. The second was Cellach, who abandoned his bishopric, and returned during his lifetime to Scotland (perhaps Ireland, but more probably the Scottish kingdom in Argyllshire). Both of these were by birth Irishmen. The third was Trumhere, by race an Englishman, but educated and ordained by the Irish." Thus Roman Christianity spread over the whole of England south of the Wash (save only heathen Sussex): while the

Irish Church had made its way over all the north, from the Wash to the Firth of Forth. The Roman influence may be partly traced by the Roman alphabet superseding the old English runes. Runic inscriptions are rare in the south, where they were regarded as heathenish relics, and so destroyed: but they are comparatively common in the north. Runics appear on the coins of the first Christian kings of Mercia, Peada and Æthelred, but soon die out under their successors.

Heathendom was now fairly vanquished. It survived only in Sussex, cut off from the rest of England by the forest belt of the Weald. The next trial of strength must clearly lie between Rome and Iona.

The northern bishops and abbots traced their succession, not to Augustine, but to Columba. Cuthberht, the English apostle of the north, who really converted the *people* of Northumbria, as earlier missionaries had converted its *kings*, derived his orders from Iona. Rome or Ireland, was now the practical question of the English Church. As might be expected, Rome conquered. To allay the discord, King Oswiu summoned a synod at Streoneshalch (now known by its later Danish name of Whitby) in 664, to settle the vexed question as to the date of Easter. The Irish priests claimed the authority of St. John for their crescent tonsure; the Romans, headed by Wilfrith, a most vigorous priest, appealed to the authority of St. Peter for the canonical circle. "I will never offend the saint who holds the keys of heaven," said Oswiu, with the frank, half-heathendom of a recent convert; and the meeting shortly decided as the king would have it. The Irish party acquiesced or else returned to Scotland; and thenceforth the new English Church remained in close communion with Rome and the Continent. Whatever may be our ecclesiastical judgment of this decision, there can be little doubt that its material effects were most excellent. By bringing England into connection with Rome, it brought her into connection with the centre of all then-existing civilisation, and endowed her with arts and manufactures which she could never otherwise have attained. The connection with Ireland and the north would have been as fatal, from a purely secular point of view, to early English culture as was the later connection with half-barbaric Scandinavia. Rome gave England the Roman letters, arts, and organisation: Ireland could only have given her a more insular form of Celtic civilisation.

* * * * *

CHAPTER XI.

CHRISTIAN ENGLAND.

The change wrought in England by the introduction of the new faith was immense and sudden at the moment, as well as deep-reaching in its after consequences. The isolated heathen barbaric communities became at once an integral part of the great Roman and Christian civilisation. Even before the arrival of Augustine, some slight tincture of Roman influence had filtered through into the English world. The Welsh serfs had preserved some traditional knowledge of Roman agriculture; Kent had kept up some intercourse with the Continent; and even in York, Eadwine affected a certain imitation of Roman pomp. But after the introduction of Christianity, Roman civilisation began to produce marked results over the whole country. Writing, before almost unknown, or confined to the engraving of runic characters on metal objects, grew rapidly into a common art. The Latin language was introduced, and with it the key to the Latin literature and Latin science, the heirlooms of Greece and the East. Roman influences affected the little courts of the English kings; and the customary laws began to be written down in regular codes. Before the conversion we have not a single written document upon which to base our history; from the moment of Augustine's landing we have the invaluable works of Bæda, and a host of lesser writings (chiefly lives of saints), besides an immense number of charters or royal grants of land to monasteries and private persons. These grants, written at first in Latin, but afterwards in Anglo-Saxon, were preserved in the monasteries down to the date of their dissolution, and then became the property of various collectors. They have been transcribed and published by Mr. Kemble and Mr. Thorpe, and they form some of our most useful materials for the early history of Christian England.

It was mainly by means of the monasteries that Christianity became a great civilising and teaching agency in England. Those who judge monastic institutions only by their later and worst days, when they had, perhaps, ceased to perform any useful function, are apt to forget the benefits which they conferred upon the people in the earlier stages of their existence. The state of England during this first Christian period was one of chronic and bloody warfare. There was no regular army, but every freeman was a soldier, and raids of one English tribe upon another were everyday occurrences; while pillaging frays on the part of the Welsh, followed by savage reprisals on the part of the English, were still more frequent. During the heathen period, even the Picts seem often to have made piratical expeditions far into the south of England. In 597, for example, we read in the Chronicle that Ceolwulf, king of the West Saxons, constantly fought "either against the English, or against the Welsh, or against the Picts." But in 603, the Argyllshire Scots made a raid against Northumbria, and were so completely crushed by Æthelfrith, that "since then no king of Scots durst lead a host against this folk"; while the southern Picts of Galloway became tributaries of the Northumbrian kings. But war between Saxons and English, or between Teutons and Welsh, still remained chronic; and Christianity did little to prevent these perpetual border wars and raids. In 633, Cadwalla and Penda wasted Northumbria; in 644, Penda drove out King Kenwealh, of the West Saxons, from his possessions along the Severn; in 671, Wulfhere, the Mercian, ravaged Wessex and the south as far as Ashdown, and conquered Wight, which he gave to the South Saxons; and so, from time to time, we catch glimpses of the unceasing strife between each folk and its neighbours, besides many hints of intestine struggles between prince and prince, or of rivalries between one petty shire and others of the same kingdom, far too numerous and unimportant to be detailed here in full.

With such a state of affairs as this, it became a matter of deep importance that there should be some one institution where the arts of peace might be carried on in safety; where agriculture might be sure of its reward; where literature and science might be studied; and where civilising influences might be safe from interruption or rapine. The monasteries gave an opportunity for such an ameliorating influence to spring up. They were spared even in war by the reverence of the people for the Church; and they became places where peaceful minds might retire for honest work, and learning, and thinking, away from the fierce turmoil of a still essentially barbaric and predatory community. At the same time, they encouraged the development of this very type of mind by turning the reproach of cowardice, which it would have carried with it in heathen times, into an honour and a mark of holiness. Every monastery became a centre of light and of struggling culture for the surrounding district. They were at once, to the early English recluse, universities and refuges, places of education, of retirement, and of peace, in the midst of a jarring and discordant world.

Hence, almost the first act of every newly-converted prince was to found a monastery in his dominions. That of Canterbury dates from the arrival of Augustine. In 643, Kenwealh of Wessex "bade timber the old minster at Winchester." In 654, shortly after the conversion of East Anglia, "Botulf began to build a monastery at Icanho," since called after his name Botulf's tun, or Boston. In 657, Peada of Mercia and Oswiu of Northumbria "said that they would rear a monastery to the glory of Christ and the honour of St. Peter; and they did so, and gave it the name of Medeshamstede"; but it is now known as Peterborough.[1]

Before the battle of Winwidfield, Oswiu had vowed to build twelve minsters in his kingdom, and he redeemed his vow by founding six in Bernicia and six in Deira. In 669, Ecgberht of Kent "gave Reculver to Bass, the mass-priest, to build a monastery thereon." In 663, Æthelthryth, a lady of royal blood, better known by the Latinised name of St. Etheldreda, "began the monastery at Ely." Before Bæda's death, in 735, religious houses already existed at Lastingham, Melrose, Lindisfarne, Whithern, Bardney, Gilling, Bury, Ripon, Chertsey, Barking, Abercorn, Selsey, Redbridge, Coldingham, Towcester, Hackness, and several other places. So the whole of England was soon covered with monastic establishments, each liberally endowed with land, and each engaged in tilling the soil without, and cultivating peaceful arts within, like little islands of southern civilisation, dotted about in the wide sea of Teutonic barbarism.

In the Roman south, many, if not all, of the monasteries seem to have been planned on the regular models; but in the north, where the Irish missionaries had borne the largest share in the work of conversion, the monasteries were irregular bodies on the Irish plan, where an abbot or abbess ruled over a mixed community of monks and nuns. Hild, a member of the Northumbrian princely family, founded such an abbey at Streoneshalch (Whitby), made memorable by numbering amongst its members the first known English poet, Cædmon. St. John of Beverley, Bishop of Hexham, set up a similar monastery at the place with which his name is so closely associated. The Irish monks themselves founded others at Lindisfarne and elsewhere. Even in the south, some Irish abbeys existed. An Irish monk had set up one at Bosham, in Sussex, even before Wilfrith converted that kingdom; and one of his countrymen, Maidulf (or Maeldubh?) was the original head of Malmesbury. In process of time, however, as the union with Rome grew stronger, all these houses conformed to the more regular usage, and became monasteries of the ordinary Benedictine type.

The civilising value of the monasteries can hardly be over-rated. Secure in the peace conferred upon them by a religious sanction, the monks became the builders of schools, the drainers of marshland, the clearers of forest, the tillers of heath. Many of the earliest religious houses rose in the midst of what had previously been trackless wilds. Peterborough and Ely grew up on islands of the Fen country. Crowland gathered round the cell of Guthlac in the midst of a desolate mere. Evesham occupied a glade in the wild forests of the western march. Glastonbury, an old Welsh foundation, stood on a solitary islet, where the abrupt knoll of the Tor looks down upon the broad waste of the Somersetshire marshes. Beverley, as its name imports, had been a haunt of beavers before the monks began to till its fruitful dingles. In every case agriculture soon turned the wild lands into orchards and cornfields, or drove drains through the fens which converted their marshes into meadows and pastures for the long-horned English cattle. Roman architecture, too, came with the Roman church. We hear nothing before of stone buildings; but Eadwine erected a church of stone at York, under the direction of Paulinus; and Bishop Wilfrith, a generation later, restored and decorated it, covering the roof with lead and filling the windows with panes of glass. Masons had already been settled in Kent, though Benedict, the founder of Wearmouth and Jarrow, found it desirable to bring over others from the Franks. Metal-working had always been a special gift of the English, and their gold jewellery was well made even before the conversion, but it became still more noticeable after the monks took the craft into their own hands. Bæda mentions mines of copper, iron, lead, silver, and jet. Abbot Benedict not only brought manuscripts and pictures from Rome, which were copied and imitated in his monasteries at Wearmouth and Jarrow, but he also brought over glass-blowers, who introduced the art of glass-making into England. Cuthberht, Bæda's scholar, writes to Lull, asking for workmen who can make glass vessels. Bells appear to have been equally early introductions. Roman music of course accompanied the Roman liturgy. The connection established with the clergy of the continent favoured the dispersion of European goods throughout England. We constantly hear of presents, consisting of skilled handicraft, passing from the civilised south to the rude and barbaric north. Wilfrith and Benedict journeyed several times to and from Rome, enlarging their own minds by intercourse with Roman society, and returning laden with works of art or manuscripts of value. Bæda was acquainted with the writings of all the chief classical poets and philosophers, whom he often quotes. We can only liken the results of such intercourse to those which in our own time have proceeded from the opening of Japan to western ideas, or of the Hawaiian Islands to European civilisation and European missionaries. The English school which soon sprang up at Rome, and the Latin schools which soon sprang up at York and Canterbury, are precise equivalents of the educational movements in both those countries which we see in our own day. The monks were to learn Latin and Greek "as well as they learned their own tongue," and were so to be given the key of all the literature and all the science that the world then possessed.

The monasteries thus became real manufacturing, agricultural, and literary centres on a small scale. The monks boiled down the salt of the brine-pits; they copied and illuminated manuscripts in the library; they painted pictures not without rude merit of their own; they ran rhines through the marshy moorland; they tilled the soil with vigour and success. A new culture began to occupy the land—the culture whose fully-developed form we now see around us. But it must never be forgotten that in its origin it is wholly Roman, and not at all Anglo-Saxon. Our people showed themselves singularly apt at embracing it, like the modern Polynesians, and unlike the American Indians; but they did not invent it for themselves. Our existing culture is not home-bred at all; it is simply the inherited and widened culture of Greece and Italy.

The most perfect picture of the monastic life and of early English Christianity which we possess is that drawn for us in the life and works of Bæda. Before giving any account, however, of the sketch which he has left us, it will be necessary to follow briefly the course of events in the English church during the few intervening years.

The Church of England in its existing form owes its organisation to a Greek monk. In 667, Oswiu of Northumbria and Ecgberht of Kent, in order to bring their dominions into closer connection with Rome, united in sending Wigheard the priest to the pope, that he might be hallowed Archbishop of Canterbury. No Englishman had yet held that office, and the choice may be regarded as a symptom of growth in the native Church. But Wigheard died at Rome, and the pope seized the opportunity to consecrate an archbishop in the Roman interest. His choice fell upon one Theodore, a monk of Tarsus in Cilicia, who was in the orders of the Eastern church. The pope was particular, however, that Theodore should not "introduce anything contrary to the verity of the faith into the Church over which he was to preside." Theodore accepted Roman orders and the Roman tonsure, and set out for his province, where he arrived after various adventures on the way. His re-organisation of the young Church was thorough and systematic. Originally England had been divided into seven great dioceses, corresponding to the principal kingdoms (save only still heathen Sussex), and having their sees in their chief towns—East and West Kent, at Canterbury and Rochester; Essex, at London; Wessex, at Dorchester or Winchester; Northumbria, at York; East Anglia, at Dunwich; and Mercia, at Lichfield. The Scottish bishopric of Lindisfarne coincided with Bernicia. Theodore divided these great dioceses into smaller ones; East Anglia had two, for its north and south folk, at Elmham and Dunwich; Bernicia was divided between Lindisfarne and Hexham; Lincolnshire had its see placed at Sidnacester; and the sub-kingdoms of Mercia were also made into dioceses, the Huiccii having their bishop-stool at Worcester; the Hecans, at Hereford; and the Middle English, at Leicester. But Theodore's great work was the establishment of the national synod, in which all the clergy of the various English kingdoms met together as a single people. This was the first step ever taken towards the unification of England; and the ecclesiastical unity thus preceded and paved the way for the political unity which was to follow it. Theodore's organisation brought the whole Church into connection with Rome. The bishops owing their orders to the Scots conformed or withdrew, and henceforward Rome held undisputed sway. Before Theodore, all the archbishops of Canterbury and all the bishops of the southern kingdoms had been Roman missionaries; those of the north had been Scots or in Scottish orders. After Theodore they were all

Englishmen in Roman orders. The native church became thenceforward wholly self-supporting.

Theodore was much aided in his projects by Wilfrith of York, a man of fiery energy and a devoted adherent of the Roman see, who had carried the Roman supremacy at the Synod of Whitby, and who spent a large part of his time in journeys between England and Italy. His life, by Ædi, forms one of the most important documents for early English history. In 681 he completed the conversion of England by his preaching to the South Saxons, whom he endeavoured to civilise as well as Christianise. His monastery of Selsey was built on land granted by the under-king (now a tributary of Wessex), and his first act was to emancipate the slaves whom he found upon the soil. Equally devoted to Rome was the young Northumbrian noble, who took the religious name of Benedict Biscop. Benedict became at first an inmate of the Abbey of Lérins, near Cannes. He afterwards founded two regular Benedictine abbeys on the same model at Wearmouth and Jarrow, and made at least four visits to the papal court, whence he returned laden with manuscripts to introduce Roman learning among his wild Northumbrian countrymen. He likewise carried over silk robes for sale to the kings in exchange for grants of land; and he brought glaziers from Gaul for his churches. Jarrow alone contained 500 monks, and possessed endowments of 15,000 acres.

It was under the walls of Jarrow that Bæda himself was born, in the year 672. Only fifty years had passed since his native Northumbria was still a heathen land. Not more than forty years had gone since the conversion of Wessex, and Sussex was still given over to the worship of Thunor and Woden. But Bæda's own life was one which brought him wholly into connection with Christian teachers and Roman culture. Left an orphan at the age of seven years, he was handed over to the care of Abbot Benedict, after whose death Abbot Ceolfrid took charge of the young aspirant. "Thenceforth," says the aged monk, fifty years later, "I passed all my lifetime in the building of that monastery [Jarrow], and gave all my days to meditating on Scripture. In the intervals of my regular monastic discipline, and of my daily task of chanting in chapel, I have always amused myself either by learning, teaching, or writing. In the nineteenth year of my life I received ordination as deacon; in my thirtieth year I attained to the priesthood; both functions being administered by the most reverend bishop John [afterwards known as St. John of Beverley], at the request of Abbot Ceolfrid. From the time of my ordination as priest to the fifty-ninth year of my life, I have occupied myself in briefly commenting upon Holy Scripture, for the use of myself and my brethren, from the works of the venerable fathers, and in some cases I have added interpretations of my own to aid in their comprehension."

The variety of Bæda's works, the large knowledge of science and of classical literature which he displays (when judged by the continental standard of the eighth century), and his familiar acquaintance with the Latin language, which he writes easily and correctly, show that the library of Jarrow must have been extensive and valuable. Besides his Scriptural commentaries, he wrote a treatise *De Natura Rerum*, Letters on the Reason of Leap-Year, a Life of St. Anastasius, and a History of his Own Abbey, all in Latin. In verse, he composed many pieces, both in hexameters and elegiacs, together with a treatise on prosody. But his greatest work is his "Ecclesiastical History of the English People," the authority from which we derive almost all our knowledge of early Christian England. It was doubtless suggested by the Frankish history of Gregory of Tours, and it consists of five books, divided into short chapters, making up about 400 pages of a modern octavo. Five manuscripts, one of them transcribed only two years after Bæda's death, and now deposited in the Cambridge library, preserve for us the text of this priceless document. The work itself should be read in the original, or in one of the many excellent translations, by every person who takes any intelligent interest in our early history.

Bæda's accomplishments included even a knowledge of Greek—then a rare acquisition in the west—which he probably derived from Archbishop Theodore's school at Canterbury. He was likewise an English author, for he translated the Gospel of St. John into his native Northumbrian; and the task proved the last of his useful life. Several manuscripts have preserved to us the letter of Cuthberht, afterwards Abbot of Jarrow, to his friend Cuthwine, giving us the very date of his death, May 27, A.D. 735, and also narrating the pathetic but somewhat overdrawn picture, with which we are all familiar, of how he died just as he had completed his translation of the last chapter. "Thus saying, he passed the day in peace till eventide. The boy [his scribe] said to him, 'Still one sentence, beloved master, is yet unwritten.' He answered, 'Write it quickly.' After a while the boy said, 'Now the sentence is written.' Then he replied, 'It is well,' quoth he, 'thou hast said the truth: it is finished.' . . . And so he passed away to the kingdom of heaven."

It is impossible to overrate the importance of the change which made such a life of earnest study and intellectual labour as Bæda's possible amongst the rough and barbaric English. Nor was it only in producing thinkers and readers from a people who could not spell a word half a century before, that the monastic system did good to England. The monasteries owned large tracts of land which they could cultivate on a co-operative plan, as cultivation was impossible elsewhere. *Laborare est orare* was the true monastic motto: and the documents of the religious houses, relating to lands and leases, show us the other or material side of the picture, which was not less important in its way than the spiritual and intellectual side. Everywhere the monks settled in the woodland by the rivers, cut down the forests, drove out the wolves and the beavers, cultivated the soil with the aid of their tenants and serfs, and became colonisers and civilisers at the same time that they were teachers and preachers. The reclamation of waste land throughout the marshes of England was due almost entirely to the monastic bodies.

The value of the civilising influence thus exerted is seen especially in the written laws, and it affected even the actions of the fierce English princes. The dooms of Æthelberht of Kent are the earliest English documents which we possess, and they were reduced to writing shortly after the conversion of the first English Christian king: while Bæda expressly mentions that they were compiled after Roman models. The Church was not able to hold the warlike princes really in check; but it imposed penances, and encouraged many of them to make pilgrimages to Rome, and to end their days in a cloister. The importance of such pilgrimages was doubtless immense. They induced the rude insular nobility to pay a visit to what was still, after all, the most civilised country of the world, and so to gain some knowledge of a foreign culture, which they afterwards endeavoured to introduce into their own homes. In 688, Ceadwalla, the ferocious king of the West Saxons, whose brother Mul had been burnt alive by the men of Kent, and who harried the Jutish kingdom in return, and who also murdered two princes of Wight, with all their people, in cold blood, went on a pilgrimage to Rome, where he was baptised, and died immediately after.[2] Ine, who succeeded him, re-endowed the old British monastery of Glastonbury, in territory just conquered from the West Welsh, and reduced the laws of the West Saxons to writing. He, too, retired to Rome, where he died. In 704, Æthelred, son of Penda, king of the Mercians, "assumed monkhood." In 709, Cenred, his successor, and Offa of Essex, went to Rome. And so on for many years, king after king resigned his kingship, and submitted, in his latter days, to the Church. Within two centuries, no less than thirty kings and queens are recorded to have embraced a conventual life: and far more probably did so, but were passed over in silence. Bæda tells us that many Englishmen went into monasteries in Gaul.

On the other hand, it cannot be denied that while Christianity made great progress, many marks of heathendom were still left among the people. Well-worship and stone-worship, devil-craft and sacrifices to idols, are mentioned in every Anglo-Saxon code of laws, and had to be provided against even as late as the time of Eadgar. The belief in elves and other semi-heathen beings, and the reverence for heathen memorials, was rife, and shows itself in such names as Ælfred, elf-counsel; Ælfstan, elf-stone; Ælfgifu, elf-given; Æthelstan, noble-stone; and Wulfstan, wolfstone. Heathendom was banished from high places, but it lingered on among the lower classes, and affected the nomenclature even of the later West Saxon kings themselves. Indeed, it was closely interwoven with all the life and thought of the people, and entered, in altered forms, even into the conceptions of Christianity current amongst them. The Christian poem of Cædmon is tinctured on every page with ideas derived from the legends of the old heathen mythology. And it will probably surprise many to learn that even at this late date, tattooing continued to be practised by the English chieftains.

1. The charter is a late forgery, but there is no reason to doubt that it represents the correct tradition.
2. He was buried at St. Peter's, and his tomb still exists in the remodelled building. Bæda quotes the inscription in full, and quotes it correctly; a fact which may be taken as an excellent test of his historical accuracy, and the care with which he collected his materials.

* * * * *

CHAPTER XII.

THE CONSOLIDATION OF THE KINGDOMS.

With the final triumph of Christianity, all the formative elements of Anglo-Saxon Britain are complete. We see it, a rough conglomeration of loosely-aggregated principalities, composed of a fighting aristocracy and a body of unvalued serfs; while interspersed through its parts are the bishops, monks, and clergy, centres of nascent civilisation for the seething mass of noble barbarism. The country is divided into agricultural colonies, and its only industry is agriculture, its only wealth, land. We want but one more conspicuous change to make it into the England of the Augustan Anglo-Saxon age—the reign of Eadgar—and that one change is the consolidation of the discordant kingdoms under a single loose over-lordship. To understand this final step, we must glance briefly at the dull record of the political history.

Under Æthelfrith, Eadwine, and Oswiu, Northumbria had been the chief power in England. But the eighth century is taken up with the greatness of Mercia. Ecgfrith, the last great king of Northumbria, whose over-lordship extended over the Picts of Galloway and the Cumbrians of Strathclyde, endeavoured to carry his conquests beyond the Forth, and annex the free land lying to the north of the old Roman line. He was defeated and slain, and with him fell the supremacy of Northumbria. Mercia, which already, under Penda and Wulfhere, had risen to the second place, now assumed the first position among the Teutonic kingdoms. Unfortunately we know little of the period of Mercian supremacy. The West Saxon chronicle contains few notices of the rival state, and we are thrown for information chiefly on the second-hand Latin historians of the twelfth century. Æthelbald, the first powerful Mercian king (716-755), "ravaged the land of the Northumbrians," and made Wessex acknowledge his supremacy. By this time all the minor kingdoms had practically become subject to the three great powers, though still retaining their native princes: and Wessex, Mercia, and Northumbria shared between them, as suzerains, the whole of Teutonic Britain. The meagre annals of the Chronicle, upon which alone (with the Charters and Latin writers of later date) we rest after the death of Bæda, show us a chaotic list of wars and battles between these three great powers themselves, or between them and their vassals, or with the Welsh and Devonians. Æthelbald was succeeded, after a short interval, by Offa, whose reign of nearly forty years (758-796), is the first settled period in English history. Offa ruled over the subject princes with rigour, and seems to have made his power really felt. He drove the Prince of Powys from Shrewsbury, and carried his ravages into the heart of Wales. He conquered the land between the Severn and the Wye, and his dyke from the Dee to the Severn, and the Wye, marked the new limits of the Welsh and English borders; while his laws codified the customs of Mercia, as those of Æthelberht and Ine had done with the customs of Kent and Wessex. He set up for awhile an archbishopric at Lichfield, which seems to mark his determination to erect Mercia into a sovereign power. He also founded the great monastery of St. Alban's, and is said to have established the English college at Rome, though another account attributes it to Ine, the West Saxon. East Anglia, Kent, Essex, and Sussex all acknowledged his supremacy. Karl the Great was then reviving the Roman Empire in its Germanic form, and Offa ventured to correspond with the Frank emperor as an equal. The possession of London, now a Mercian city, gave Offa an interest in continental affairs; and the growth of trade is marked by the fact that when a quarrel arose between them, they formally closed the ports of their respective kingdoms against each other's subjects.

Nevertheless, English kingship still remained a mere military office, and consolidation, in our modern sense, was clearly impossible. Local jealousies divided all the little kingdoms and their component principalities; and any real subordination was impracticable amongst a purely agricultural and warlike people, with no regular army, and governed only by their own anarchic desires. Like the Afghans of the present time, the early English were incapable of union, except in a temporary way under the strong hand of a single warlike leader against a common foe. As soon as that was removed, they fell asunder at once into their original separateness. Hence the chaotic nature of our early annals, in which it is impossible to discover any real order underlying the perpetual flux of states and princes.

A single story from the Chronicle will sufficiently illustrate the type of men whose actions make up the history of these predatory times. In 754, King Cuthred of the West Saxons died. His kinsman, Sigeberht, succeeded him. One year later, however, Cynewulf and the witan deprived Sigeberht of his kingdom, making over to him only the petty principality of Hampshire, while Cynewulf himself reigned in his stead. After a time Sigeberht murdered an ealdorman of his suite named Cymbra; whereupon Cynewulf deprived him of his remaining territory and drove him forth into the forest of the Weald. There he lived a wild life till a herdsman met him in the forest and stabbed him, to avenge the death of his master, Cymbra. Cynewulf, in turn, after spending his days in fighting the Welsh, lost his life in a quarrel with Cyneheard, brother of the outlawed Sigeberht. He had endeavoured to drive out the ætheling; but Cyneheard surprised him at Merton, and slew him with all his thegns, except one Welsh hostage. Next day, the king's friends, headed by the ealdorman Osric, fell upon the ætheling, and killed him with all his followers. In the very same year, Æthelbald of Mercia was killed fighting at Seckington; and Offa drove out his successor, Beornred. Of such murders, wars, surprises, and dynastic quarrels, the history of the eighth century is full. But no modern reader need know more of them than the fact that they existed, and that they prove the wholly ungoverned and ungovernable nature of the early English temper.

Until the Danish invasions of the ninth century, the tribal kingdoms still remained practically separate, and such cohesion as existed was only secured for the purpose of temporary defence or aggression. Essex kept its own kings under Æthelberht of Kent; Huiccia retained its royal house under Æthelred of Mercia; and later on, Mercia itself had its ealdormen, after the conquest by Ecgberht of Wessex. Each royal line reigned under the supreme power until it died out naturally, like our own great feudatories in India at the present day. "When Wessex and Mercia have worked their way to the rival hegemonies," says Canon Stubbs, "Sussex and Essex do not cease to be numbered among the kingdoms, until their royal houses are extinct. When Wessex has conquered Mercia and brought Northumbria on its knees, there are still kings in both Northumbria and Mercia. The royal house of Kent dies out, but the title of King of Kent is bestowed on an ætheling, first of the Mercian, then of the West Saxon house. Until the Danish conquest, the dependant royalties seem to have been spared; and even afterwards organic union can scarcely be said to exist."

The final supremacy of the West Saxons was mainly brought about by the Danish invasion. But the man who laid the foundation of the West Saxon power was Ecgberht, the so-called first king of all England. Banished from Wessex during his youth by one of the constant dynastic quarrels, through the enmity of Offa, the young ætheling had taken refuge with Karl the Great, at the court of Aachen, and there had learnt to understand the rising statesmanship of the Frankish race and of the restored Roman empire. The death of his enemy Beorhtric, in 802, left the kingdom open to him: but the very day of his accession showed him the character of the people whom he had come to rule. The men of Worcester celebrated his arrival by a raid on the men of Wilts. "On that ilk day," says the Chronicle, "rode Æthelhund, ealdorman of the Huiccias [who were Mercians], over at Cynemæres ford; and there Weohstan the ealdorman met him with the Wilts men [who were West Saxons:] and there was a muckle fight, and both ealdormen were slain, and the Wilts men won the day." For twenty years, Ecgberht was engaged in consolidating his ancestral dominions: but at the end of that time, he found himself able to attack the Mercians, who had lost Offa six years before Ecgberht's return. In 825, the West Saxons met the Mercian host at Ellandun, "and Ecgberht gained the day, and there was muckle slaughter." Therefore all the Saxon name, held tributary by the Mercians, gathered about the Saxon champion. "The Kentish folk, and they of Surrey, and the South Saxons, and the East Saxons turned to him." In the same year, the East Anglians, anxious to avoid the power of Mercia, "sought Ecgberht for peace and for aid." Beornwulf, the Mercian king, marched against his revolted tributaries: but the East Anglians fought him stoutly, and slew him and his successor in two battles. Ecgberht followed up this step by annexing Mercia in 829: after which he marched northward against the Northumbrians, who at once "offered him obedience and peace; and they thereupon parted." One year later, Ecgberht led an army against the northern Welsh, and "reduced them to humble obedience." Thus the West Saxon kingdom absorbed all the others, at least so far as a loose over-lordship was concerned. Ecgberht had rivalled his master Karl by founding, after a fashion, the empire of the English. But all the local jealousies smouldered on as fiercely as ever, the under-kings retained their several dominions, and Ecgberht's supremacy was merely one of superior force, unconnected with any real organic unity of the kingdom as a whole. Ecgberht himself generally bore the title of King of the West Saxons, like his ancestors: and though in dealing with his Anglian subjects he styled himself Rex Anglorum, that title perhaps means little more than the humbler one of Rex Gewissorum, which he used in addressing his people of the lesser principality. The real kingdom of the English never existed before the days of Eadward the Elder, and scarcely before the days of William the Norman and Henry the Angevin. As to the kingdom of England, that was a far later invention of the feudal lawyers.

* * * * *

CHAPTER XIII.

THE RESISTANCE TO THE DANES.

In the long period of three and a-half centuries which had elapsed between the Jutish conquest of Kent and the establishment of the West Saxon over-lordship, the politics of Britain had been wholly insular. The island had been brought back by Augustine and his successors into ecclesiastical, commercial, and literary union with the continent: but no foreign war or invasion had ever broken the monotony of murdering the Welsh and harrying the surrounding English. The isolation of England was complete. Ship-building was almost an obsolete art: and the small trade which still centred in London seems to have been mainly carried on in Frisian bottoms; for the Low Dutch of the continent still retained the seafaring habits which those of England had forgotten. But a new enemy was now beginning to appear in northern Europe—the Scandinavians. The history of the great wicking movement forms the subject of a separate volume in this series: but the manner in which the English met it will demand a brief treatment here. Some outline of the bare facts, however, must first be premised.

As early as 789, during the reign of Offa in Mercia, "three ships of Northmen from Hæretha land" came on shore in Wessex. "Then the reeve rode against them, and would have driven them to the king's town, for he wist not what they were: and there men slew him. Those were the first ships of Danish men that ever sought English kin's land." In 795, "the harrying of heathen men wretchedly destroyed God's church at Lindisfarne isle, through rapine and manslaughter." In the succeeding year, "the heathen harried among the Northumbrians, and plundered Ecgberht's monastery at Wearmouth." In 832, "heathen men ravaged Sheppey"; and a year later, "King Ecgberht fought against the crews of thirty-five ships at Charmouth, and there was muckle slaughter made, and the Danes held the battle-field."[1] In 835, another host came to the West Welsh (now almost reduced to the peninsula of Cornwall): and the Welsh readily joined them against their West Saxon over-lord. Ecgberht met the united hosts at Hengestesdun and put them both to flight. It was his last success. In the succeeding year he died, and the kingdom descended to his weak son, Æthelwulf. His second son, Æthelstan, was placed over Kent, Essex, Surrey, and Sussex, as under-king.

Next spring, the flood of wickings began to pour in earnest over England. Thirty-three piratical ships sailed up Southampton Water to pillage Southampton, perhaps with an ultimate eye to the treasures of royal Winchester, the capital and minster-town of the West Saxon over-lord himself. This was a bold attempt, but the West Saxons met it in full force. The ealdorman Wulfheard gathered together the levy of fighting men, attacked the host, and put it to flight with great slaughter. Shortly after a second Danish host landed near Portland, doubtless to plunder Dorchester: and the local ealdorman Æthelhelm, falling upon them with the levy of Dorset men, was defeated after a sharp struggle, leaving the heathen in possession of the field. It was not in Wessex, however, that the wickings were to make their great success. The north had long suffered from terrible anarchy, and was a ready prey for any invader. Out of fourteen kings who had reigned in Northumbria during the eighth century, no less than seven were put to death and six expelled by their rebellious subjects. Christian Northumbria, which in Bæda's days had been the most flourishing part of Britain, was now reduced to a mere agglomeration of petty princes and clans, dependent on the West Saxon over-lord, and utterly unconnected with one another in feeling or sympathy. Already we have seen how the Danes harried Northumbria without opposition. The same was probably the case with the whole Anglian coast on the east. In 840, the wickings fell on the fen country. "The ealdorman Hereberht was slain by heathen men, and many with him among the marsh-men." All down the east coast, the piratical fleet proceeded, burning and slaughtering as it went. "In the same year, in Lindsey, and in East Anglia, and among the Kent men, many men were slain by the host." A year later, the wickings returned, growing bolder as they found out the helplessness of the people. They sailed up the Thames, and ravaged Rochester and London, with great slaughter; after which they crossed the channel and fell upon Cwantawic, or Étaples, a commercial port in the Saxon land of the Boulonnais. In 842, a Danish host defeated Æthelwulf himself at Charmouth in Dorset; and in the succeeding summer "the ealdorman Eanulf, with the Somerset levy, and Bishop Ealhstan and the ealdorman Osric, with the Dorset levy, fought at Parretmouth with the host, and made a muckle slaughter, and won the day."

The utter weakness of the first English resistance is well shown in these facts. A terrible flood of heathen savagery was let loose upon the country, and the people were wholly unable to cope with it. There was absolutely no central organisation, no army, no commissariat, no ships. The heathen host landed suddenly wherever it found the people unprepared, and fell upon the larger towns for plunder. The local authority, the ealdorman or the under-king, hastily gathered together the local levy in arms, and fell upon the pirates tumultuously with the men of the shire as best he might. But he had no provisions for a long campaign: and when the levy had fought once, it melted away immediately, every man going back again of necessity to his own home. If it won the battle, it went home to drink over its success: if it lost, it dissolved, demoralized, and left the burghers to fight for their own walls, or to buy off the heathen with their own money. But every shire and every kingdom fought for itself alone. If the Dorset men could only drive away the host from Charmouth and Portland, they cared little whether it sailed away to harry Sussex and

Hants. If the Northumbrians could only drive it away from the Humber, they cared little whether it set sail for the Thames and the Solent. The North Folk of East Anglia were equally happy to send it off toward the South Folk. While there was so little cohesion between the parts of the same kingdoms, there was no cohesion at all between the different kingdoms over which Æthelwulf exercised a nominal over-lordship. The West Saxon kings fought for Dorset and for Kent, but there is no trace of their ever fighting for East Anglia or for Northumbria. They left their northern vassals to take care of themselves. "It was never a war between the Danes and the national army," says Prof. Pearson, "but between the Danes and a local militia." It would have been impossible, indeed, to resist the wickings effectually without a strong central system, which could move large armies rapidly from point to point: and such a system was quite undreamt of in the half-consolidated England of the ninth century. Only war with a foreign invader could bring it about even in a faint degree: and that was exactly what the Danish invasion did for Wessex.

The year 851 marks an important epoch in the English resistance. The annual horde of wickings had now become as regular in its recurrence as summer itself; and even the inert West Saxon kings began to feel that permanent measures must be taken against them. They had built ships, and tried to tackle the invaders in the only way in which so partially civilised a race could tackle such tactics as those of the Danes—upon the sea. A host of wickings came round to Sandwich in Kent. The under-king Æthelstan fell upon them with his new navy, and took nine of their ships, putting the rest to flight with great slaughter. But in the same year another great host of 250 sail, by far the largest fleet of which we have yet heard, came to the mouth of the Thames, and there landed, a step which marks a fresh departure in the wicking tactics. They took Canterbury by assault, and then marched on to London. There they stormed the busy merchant town, and put to flight Beorhtwulf, the under-king of the Mercians, with his local levy. Thence they proceeded southward into Surrey, doubtless on their way to Winchester. King Æthelwulf met them at Ockley, with the West-Saxon levy, "and there made the greatest slaughter among the heathen host that we have yet heard, and gained the day." In spite of these two great successes, however, both of which show an increasing statesmanship on the part of the West Saxons, this year was memorable in another way, for "the heathen men for the first time sat over winter in Thanet." The loose predatory excursions were beginning to take the complexion of regular conquest and permanent settlement.

Yet so little did the English still realise the terrible danger of the heathen invasion, that next year Æthelwulf was fighting the Welsh of Wales; and two years after he went on a pilgrimage to Rome, "with great pomp, and dwelt there twelve months, and then fared homeward." In that same year, "heathen men sat over winter in Sheppey."

After Æthelwulf's death the English resistance grew fainter and fainter. In 860, under his second son, Æthelberht, a Danish host took Winchester itself by storm. Five years later, a heathen army settled in Thanet, and the men of Kent agreed to buy peace of them—the first sign of that evil habit of buying off the Dane, which grew gradually into a fixed custom. But the host stole away during the truce for collecting the money, and harried all Kent unawares.

Meanwhile, we hear little of the North. The almost utter destruction of its records during the heathen domination restricts us for information to the West Saxon chronicles; and they have little to tell us about any but their own affairs. In 866, however, we learn that there came a great heathen host to East Anglia—an organised expedition under two chieftains—"and took winter quarters there, and were horsed; and the East Anglians made peace with them." Next year, this permanent host sailed northward to Humber, and attacked York. The Northumbrians, as usual, were at strife among themselves, two rival kings fighting for the supremacy. The burghers of York admitted the heathen host within the walls. Then the rival kings fell upon the town, broke the slender fortifications, and rushed into the city. The Danes attacked them both, and defeated them with great slaughter. Northumbria passed at once into the power of the heathen. Their chiefs, Ingvar and Ubba, erected Deira into a new Danish kingdom, leaving Bernicia to an English puppet; and Northumbria ceases to exist for the present as a factor in Anglo-Saxon history. We must hand it over for sixty years to the Scandinavian division of this series.

In 868, Ingvar and Ubba advanced again into Mercia and beset Nottingham. Then the under-king Burhred called in the aid of his over-lord, Æthelred of Wessex, who came to his assistance with a levy. "But there was no hard fight there, and the Mercians made peace with the host." In 870, the heathen overran East Anglia, and destroyed the great monastery of Peterborough, probably the richest religious house in all England. Eadmund, the under-king, came against them with the levy, but they slew him; and the people held him for a martyr, whose shrine at Bury St. Edmunds grew in after days into the holiest spot in East Anglia. The Danes harried the whole country, burnt the monasteries, and annexed Norfolk and Suffolk as a second Danish kingdom. East Anglia, too, disappears for a while from our English annals.

Lastly, the Danes turned against Mercia and Wessex. In 871, a host under Bagsecg and Halfdene came to Reading, which belonged to the latter territory, when the local ealdorman engaged them and won a slight victory. Shortly afterward the West Saxon king Æthelred, with his brother Ælfred, came up, and engaged them a second time with worse success. Three other bloody battles followed, in all of which the Danes were beaten with heavy loss; but the West Saxons also suffered severely. For three years the host moved up and down through Mercia and Wessex; and the Mercians stood by, aiding neither side, but "making peace with the host" from time to time. At last, however, in 874, the heathens finally annexed the greater part of Mercia itself. "The host fared from Lindsey to Repton, and there sat for the winter, and drove King Burhred over sea, two and twenty years after he came to the kingdom; and they subdued all the land. And Burhred went to Rome, and there settled; and his body lies in St. Mary's Church, in the school of the English kin. And in the same year they gave the kingdom of Mercia in ward to Ceolwulf, an unwise thegn; and he swore oaths to them, and gave hostages that it should be ready for them on whatso day they willed; and that he would be ready with his own body, and with all who would follow him, for the behoof of the host." Thus Mercia, too, fades for a short while out of our history, and Wessex alone of all the English kingdoms remains.

This brief but inevitable record of wars and battles is necessarily tedious, yet it cannot be omitted without slurring over some highly important and interesting facts. It is impossible not to be struck with the extraordinarily rapid way in which a body of fierce heathen invaders overran two great Christian and comparatively civilised states. We cannot but contrast the inertness of Northumbria and the lukewarmness of Mercia with the stubborn resistance finally made by Ælfred in Wessex. The contrast may be partly due, it is true, to the absence of native Northumbrian and Mercian accounts. We might, perhaps, find, had we fuller details, that the men of Bernicia and Deira made a harder fight for their lands and their churches than the West Saxon annals would lead us to suppose. Still, after making all allowance for the meagreness of our authorities, there remains the indubitable fact that a heathen kingdom was established in the pure English land of Bæda and Cuthberht, while the Christian faith and the Saxon nationality held their own for ever in peninsular and half-Celtic Wessex.

The difference is doubtless due in part to merely surface causes. East Anglia had long lost her autonomy, and, while sometimes ruled by Mercia, was sometimes broken up under several ealdormen. For her and for Northumbria the conquest was but a change from a West Saxon to a Danish master. The house of Ecgberht had broken down the national and tribal organisation, and was incapable of substituting a central organisation in its place. With no roads and no communications such a centralising scheme is really impracticable. The disintegrated English kingdoms made little show of fighting for their Saxon over-lord. They could accept a Dane for master almost as readily as they could accept a Saxon.

But besides these surface causes, there was a deeper and more fundamental cause underlying the difference. The Scandinavians were nearer to the pure English in blood and speech than they were to the Saxons. In their old home the two races had lived close together,—in Sleswick, Jutland, and Scania,—while the Saxons had dwelt further south, near the Frankish border, by the lowlands of the Elbe. To the English of Northumbria, the Saxons of Wessex were almost foreigners. Even at the present day, when the existence of a recognised literary dialect has done so much to obliterate provincial varieties of speech in England, a Dorsetshire peasant, speaking in a slightly altered form the classical West Saxon of Ælfred, has great difficulty in understanding a Yorkshire peasant, speaking in a slightly altered form the classical Northumbrian of Bæda. But in the ninth century the differences between the two dialects were probably far greater. On the other hand, though Danish and Anglian have widely separated at the present day, and were widely distinct even in the days of Cnut, it is probable that at this earlier period they were still, to some extent, mutually comprehensible. Thus, the heathen Scandinavian may have seemed to the Northumbrian and the East Anglian almost like a fellow-countryman, while the West Saxon seemed in part like an enemy and an intruder. At any rate, the similarity of blood and language enabled the two races rapidly to coalesce; and when the cloud rises again from the North half a century later, the distinction of Dane and Englishman has almost ceased in the conquered provinces. It is worthy of note in this connection that the part of Mercia afterwards given over by Ælfred to Guthrum, was the Anglian half, while the part retained by Wessex was mostly the Saxon half—the land conquered by Penda from the West Saxons two hundred years before.

Nor must we suppose that this first wave of Scandinavian conquest in any way swamped or destroyed the underlying English population of the North. The conquerors came merely as a "host," or army of occupation, not as a body of rural colonists. They left the conquered English in possession of their homes, though they seized upon the manors for themselves, and kept the higher dignities of the vanquished provinces in their own hands. Being rapidly converted to Christianity, they amalgamated readily with the native people. Few women came over with them, and intermarriage with the English soon broke down the wall of separation. The archbishopric of York continued its succession uninterruptedly throughout the Danish occupation. The Bishops of Elmham lived through the stormy period; those of Leicester transferred their see to Dorchester-on-the-Thames; those of Lichfield apparently kept up an unbroken series. We may gather that beneath the surface the North remained just as steadily English under the Danish princes as the whole country afterwards remained steadily English under the Norman kings.

There was, however, one section of the true English race which kept itself largely free from the Scandinavian host. North of the Tyne the Danes apparently spread but sparsely; English ealdormen continued to rule at Bamborough over the land between Forth and Tyne. Hence Northumberland and the Lothians remained more purely English than any other part of Britain. The people of the South are Saxons: the people of the West are half Celts; the people of the North and the Midlands are largely intermixed with Danes; but the people of the Scottish lowlands, from Forth to Tweed, are almost purely English; and the dialect which we always describe as Scotch is the strongest, the tersest, and the most native modern form of the original Anglo-Saxon tongue. If we wish to find the truest existing representative of the genuine pure-blooded English race, we must look for him, not in Mercia or in Wessex, but amongst the sturdy and hard-headed farmers of Tweedside and Lammermoor.

1. This entry in the Chronicle, however, is probably erroneous, as an exactly similar one occurs under Æthelwulf, seven years later.

* * * * *

CHAPTER XIV.

THE SAXONS AT BAY IN WESSEX.

Only one English kingdom now held out against the wickings, and that was Wessex. Its comparatively successful resistance may be set down, in some slight degree, to the energy of a single man, Ælfred, though it was doubtless far more largely due to the relatively strong organisation of the West Saxon state. In judging of Ælfred, we must lay aside the false notions derived from the application of words expressing late ideas to an early and undeveloped stage of civilised society. To call him a great general or a great statesman is to use utterly misleading terms. Generalship and statesmanship, as we understand them, did not yet exist, and to speak of them in the ninth century in England is to be guilty of a common, but none the more excusable, anachronism. Ælfred was a sturdy and hearty fighter, and a good king of a semi-barbaric people. As a lad, he had visited Rome; and he retained throughout life a strong sense of his own and his people's barbarism, and a genuine desire to civilise himself and his subjects, so far as his limited lights could carry him. He succeeded to a kingdom overrun from end to end by piratical hordes: and he did his best to restore peace and to promote order. But his character was merely that of a practical, common-sense, fighting West Saxon, brought up in the camp of his father and brothers, and doing his rough work in life with the honest straightforwardness of a simple, hard-headed, religious, but only half-educated barbaric soldier.

The successful East Anglian wickings, under their chief Guthrum, turned at once to ravage Wessex. They "harried the West Saxons' land, and settled there, and drove many of the folk over sea." For awhile it seemed as if Wessex too was to fall into their hands. Ælfred himself, with a little band, "withdrew to the woods and moor-fastnesses." He took refuge in the Somerset marshes, and there occupied a little island of dry land in the midst of the fens, by name Athelney. Here he threw up a rude earthwork, from which he made raids against the Danes, with a petty levy of the nearest Somerset men. But the mass of the West Saxons were not disposed to give in so easily. The long border warfare with Devon and Cornwall had probably kept up their organisation in a better state than that of the anarchic North. The men of Somerset and Wilts, with those Hampshire men who had not fled to the Continent, gathered at a sacred stone on the borders of Selwood Forest, and there Ælfred met them with his little band. They attacked the host, which they put to flight, and then besieged it in its fortified camp. To escape the siege, Guthrum consented to leave Wessex, and to accept Christianity. He was baptised at once, with thirty of his principal chiefs, after the rough-and-ready fashion of the fighting king, near Athelney. The treaty entered into with Guthrum restored to Ælfred all Wessex, with the south-western part of Mercia, from London to Bedford, and thence along the line of Watling Street to Chester. Thus for a time the Saxons recovered their autonomy, and the great Scandinavian horde retired to East Anglia. Æthelred, Ælfred's son-in-law, was appointed under-king of recovered Mercia. Henceforward, Teutonic Britain remains for awhile divided into Wessex and the Denalagu—that is to say, the district governed by Danish law.

Though peace was thus made with Guthrum, new bodies of wickings came pouring southward from Scandinavia. One of these sailed up the Thames to Fulham, but after spending some time there, they went over to the Frankish coast, where their depredations were long and severe. Throughout all Ælfred's reign, with only two intervals of peace, the wickings kept up a constant series of attacks on the coast, and frequently penetrated inland. From time to time, the great horde under Hæsten poured across the country, cutting the corn and driving away the cattle, and retreating into East Anglia, or Northumbria, or the peninsula of the Wirrall, whenever they were seriously worsted. "Thanks be to God," says the Chronicle pathetically "the host had not wholly broken up all the English kin;" but the misery of England must have been intense. Ælfred, however, introduced two military changes of great importance. He set on foot something like a regular army, with a settled commissariat, dividing his forces into two bodies, so that one-half was constantly at home tilling the soil while the other half was in the field; and he built large ships on a new plan, which he manned with Frisians, as well as with English, and which largely aided in keeping the coast fairly free from Danish invasion during the two intervals of peace.

Throughout the whole of the ninth century, however, and the early part of the tenth, the whole history of England is the history of a perpetual pillage. No man who sowed could tell whether he might reap or not. The Englishman lived in constant fear of life and goods; he was liable at any moment to be called out against the enemy. Whatever little civilisation had ever existed in the country died out almost altogether. The Latin language was forgotten even by the priests. War had turned everybody into fighters; commerce was impossible when the towns were sacked year after year by the pirates. But in the rare intervals of peace, Ælfred did his best to civilise his people. The amount of work with which he is credited is truly astonishing. He translated into English with his own hand "The History of the World," by Orosius; Bæda's "Ecclesiastical History;" Boethius's "De Consolatione," and Gregory's "Regula Pastoralis." At his court, too, if not under his own direction, the English Chronicle was first begun, and many of the sentences quoted from that great document in this work are probably due to Ælfred himself. His devotion to the church was shown by the regular communication which he kept up with Rome, and by the gifts which he sent from his impoverished kingdom, not only to the shrine of St. Peter but even to that of St. Thomas in India. No doubt his vigorous personality counted for much in the struggle with the Danes; but his death in 901 left the West Saxons as ready as ever to contend against the northern enemy.

One result of the Danish invasion of Wessex must not be passed over. The common danger seems to have firmly welded together Welshman and Saxon into a single nationality. The most faithful part of Ælfred's dominions were the West Welsh shires of Somerset and Devon, with the half Celtic folk of Dorset and Wilts. The result is seen in the change which comes over the relations between the two races. In Ine's laws the distinction between Welshmen and Englishmen is strongly marked; the price of blood for the servile population is far less than that of their lords: in Ælfred's laws the distinction has died out. Compared to the heathen Dane, West Saxons and West Welsh were equally Englishmen. From that day to this, the Celtic peasantry of the West Country have utterly forgotten their Welsh kinship, save in wholly Cymric Cornwall alone. The Devon and Somerset men have for centuries been as English in tongue and feeling as the people of Kent or Sussex.

* * * * *

CHAPTER XV.

THE RECOVERY OF THE NORTH.

The history of the tenth century and the first half of the eleventh consists entirely of the continued contest between the West Saxons and the Scandinavians. It falls naturally into three periods. The first is that of the English reaction, when the West Saxon kings, Eadward and Æthelstan, gradually reconquered the Danish North by inches at a time. The second is that of the Augustan age, when Dunstan and Eadgar held together the whole of Britain for a while in the hands of a single West Saxon over-lord. The third is that of the decadence, when, under Æthelred, the ill-welded empire fell asunder, and the Danish kings, Cnut, Harold, and Harthacnut, ruled over all England, including even the unconquered Wessex of Ælfred himself.

At Ælfred's death, his dominions comprised the larger Wessex, from Kent to the Cornish border at Exeter, together with the portion of Mercia south-west of Watling Street. The former kingdom passed into the hands of his son Eadward; the latter was still held by the ealdorman Æthelred, who had married Ælfred's daughter Æthelflæd. The departure of the Danish host, led by Hæsten, left the English time to breathe and to recruit their strength. Henceforth, for nearly a century, the direct wicking incursions cease, and the war is confined to a long struggle with the Northmen already settled in England. Four years later, the east Anglian Danes broke the peace and harried Mercia and Wessex; but Eadward overran their lands in return, and the Kentish men, in a separate battle, attacked and slew Eric their king with several of his earls. In 912, Æthelred the Mercian died, and Eadward at once incorporated London and Oxford with his own dominions, leaving his sister Æthelflæd only the northern half of her husband's principality. Thenceforth Æthelflæd, "the Lady of the Mercians," turned deliberately to the conquest of the North. She adopted a fresh kind of tactics, which mark again a new departure in the English policy. Instead of keeping to the old plan of alternate harryings on either side, and precarious tenure of lands from time to time, Æthelflæd began building regular fortresses or *burhs* all along her north-eastern frontiers, using these afterwards as bases for fresh operations against the enemy. The spade went hand in hand with the sword: the English were becoming engineers as well as fighters. In the year of her husband's death, the Lady built *burhs* at Sarrat and Bridgnorth. The next year "she went with all the Mercians to Tamworth, and built the *burh* there in early summer; and ere Lammas, that at Stafford." In the two succeeding years she set up other strongholds at Eddesbury, Warwick, Cherbury, Wardbury, and Runcorn. By 917, she found herself strong enough to attack Derby, one of the chief cities in the Danish confederacy of the Five Burgs, which she captured after a hard siege. Thence she turned on Leicester, which capitulated on her approach, the Danish host going over quietly to her side. She was in communication with the Danes of York for the surrender of that city, too, when she died suddenly in her royal town of Tamworth, in the year 918.

Meanwhile Eadward had been pushing forward his own boundary in the east, building *burhs* at Hertford and Witham, and endeavouring to subjugate the Danish league in Bedford, Huntingdon, and Northampton. In 915, Thurketel, the jarl of Bedford, "sought him for lord," and Eadward afterwards built a *burh* there also. On his sister's death, he annexed all her territories, and then, in a fierce and long doubtful struggle, reconquered not only Huntingdon and Northampton but East Anglia as well. The Christian English hailed him as a deliverer. Next, he turned on Stamford, the Danish capital of the Fens, and on Nottingham, the stronghold of the Southumbrian host. In both towns he erected *burhs*. These successes once more placed the West Saxon king in the foremost position amongst the many rulers of Britain. The smaller principalities, unable to hold their own against the Scandinavians, began spontaneously to rally round Eadward as their leader and suzerain. In the same year with the conquest of Stamford, "the kings of the North Welsh, Howel, and Cledauc, and Jeothwel, and all the North Welsh kin, sought him for lord." In 923, Eadward pushed further northward, and sent a Mercian host to conquer "Manchester in Northumbria," and fortify and man it. A line of twenty fortresses now girdled the English frontier, from Colchester, through Bedford and Nottingham, to Manchester and Chester. Next year, Eadward himself, now immediate king of all England south of Humber, attacked the last remaining Danish kingdom, Northumbria, throwing a bridge across the Trent at Nottingham, and marching against Bakewell in Peakland, where again he built a *burh*. The new tactics were too fine for the rough and ready Danish leaders. Before Eadward reached York, the entire North submitted without a blow. "The king of Scots, and all the Scottish kin, and Ragnald [Danish king of York], and the sons of Eadulf [English kings of Bamborough], and all who dwell in Northumbria, as well English as Danes and Northmen and others, and also the king of the Strathclyde Welsh and all the Strathclyde Welsh, sought him for father and for lord." This was in 924. Next year, Eadward "rex invictus" died, over-lord of all Britain from sea to sea, while the whole country south of the Humber, save only Wales and Cornwall, was now practically united into a single kingdom of England.

But the seeming submission of the North was fallacious. The Danes had reintroduced into Britain a fresh mass of incoherent barbarism, which could not thus readily coalesce. The Scandinavian leaven in the population had put back the shadow on the dial of England some three centuries. Æthelstan, Eadward's son, found himself obliged to give his sister in marriage to Sihtric or Sigtrig, Danish king of the Yorkshire Northumbrians, which probably marks a recognition of his vassal's equality. Soon after, however, Sihtric died, and Æthelstan made himself first king of all England by adding Northumbria to his own immediate dominions. Then "he bowed to himself all the kings who were in this island; first, Howel, king of the West Welsh; and Constantine, king of Scots; and Owen, king of Gwent [South Wales]; and Ealdred, son of Ealdulf of Bamborough; and with pledge and with oaths sware they peace, and forsook every kind of heathendom." In the West, he drove the Welsh from Exeter, which they had till then occupied in common with the English, and fixed their boundary at the Tamar. But once more the pretended vassals rebelled. Constantine, king of Scots, threw off his allegiance, and Æthelstan thereupon "went into Scotland, both with a land host and a ship host, and harried a mickle deal of it." In 937, the feudatories made a final and united effort to throw off the West Saxon yoke. The Scots, the Strathclyde Welsh, the people of Wales and Cornwall, the lords of Bamborough, and the Danes throughout the North and East, all rose together in a great league against their over-lord. Anlaf, king of the Dublin Danes, came over from Ireland to aid them, with a large body of wickings. The confederates met the West Saxon *fyrd* or levy at an unknown spot named Brunanburh, where Æthelstan overthrew them in a crushing defeat, which forms the subject of a fine war-song, inserted in full in the English Chronicle.[1] Three years later Æthelstan died, as his father had died before him, undisputed over-lord of all Britain, and immediate king of the whole Teutonic portion.

Yet once more the feeble unity of the country broke hopelessly asunder. Eadmund, who succeeded his brother, found the Danes of the North and the Midlands again insubordinate. The year after his accession "the Northumbrians belied their oath, and chose Anlaf of Ireland for king." The Five Burgs went too, and the old boundary of Watling Street was once more made the frontier of the Danish possessions. In 944, however, Eadmund subdued all Northumbria, and expelled its Danish kings. His recovery of the Five Burgs, and the joy of the Christian English inhabitants, are vividly set forth in a fragmentary ballad embedded in the Chronicle. The next year he harried Strathclyde or Cumberland, the Welsh kingdom between Clyde and Morecambe, and handed it over to Malcolm, king of Scots, as a pledge of his fidelity. At Eadmund's death in 946—when he was stabbed in his royal hall by an outlaw—his kingdom fell to his brother Eadred. Two years later Northumbria again revolted, and chose Eric for its king. Eadred harried and burnt the province, which he then handed over to an earl of his own creation, one of the Bamborough family. The king himself died in 955, and was succeeded by his nephew Eadwig. But Northumbria and Mercia revolted once more, and chose Eadwig's brother, Eadgar, instead of their own Danish princes. Eadwig died in 958, and Eadgar then became king of all three provinces; thus finally uniting the whole of Teutonic England into one kingdom.

Eadgar's reign forms the climax of the West Saxon power. It was, in fact, the only period when England can be said to have enjoyed any national unity under the Anglo-Saxon dynasties. The strong hand of a priest gave peace for some years to the ill-organised mass. Dunstan was probably the first Englishman who seriously deserves the name of statesman. He was born in the half-Celtic region of Somerset, beside the great abbey of Glastonbury, which held the bones of Arthur, and a good deal of the imaginative Celtic temper ran probably with the blood in his veins.[2] But he was above all the representative of the Roman civilisation in the barbarised, half-Danish England of the tenth century. He was a musician, a painter, a reader, and a scholar, in a world of fierce warriors and ignorant nobles. Eadmund made him abbot of Glastonbury. Eadgar appointed him first bishop of London, and then, on Eadwig's death, Archbishop of Canterbury. It was Dunstan who really ruled England throughout the remainder of his life. Essentially an organiser and administrator, he was able to weld the unwieldy empire into a rough unity, which lasted as long as its author lived, and no longer. He appeased the discontent of Northumbria and the Five Burgs by permitting them a certain amount of local independence, with the enjoyment of their own laws and their own lawmen. He kept a fleet of boats cruising in the Irish Sea to check the

Danish hosts at Dublin and Waterford. He put forward a code, known as the laws of Eadgar, for the better government of Wessex and the South. He made the over-lordship of the West Saxons over their British vassals more real than it had ever been before; and a tale, preserved by Florence, tells us that eight tributary kings rowed Eadgar in his royal barge on the Dee, in token of their complete subjection. Internally, Dunstan revived the declining spirit of monasticism, which had died down during the long struggle with the Danes, and attempted to reintroduce some tinge of southern civilisation into the barbarised and half-paganised country in which he lived. Wherever it was possible, he "drove out the priests, and set monks," and he endeavoured to make the monasteries, which had degenerated during the long war into mere landowning communities, regain once more their old position as centres of culture and learning. During his own time his efforts were successful, and even after his death the movement which he had begun continued in this direction to make itself felt, though in a feebler and less intelligent form.

One act of Dunstan's policy, however, had far-reaching results, of a kind which he himself could never have anticipated. He handed over all Northumbria beyond the Tweed—the region now known as the Lothians—as a fief to Kenneth, king of Scots. This accession of territory wholly changed the character of the Scottish kingdom, and largely promoted the Teutonisation of the Celtic North. The Scottish princes now took up their residence in the English town of Edinburgh, and learned to speak the English language as their mother-tongue. Already Eadmund had made over Strathclyde or Cumberland to Malcolm; and thus the dominions of the Scottish kings extended over the whole of the country now known as Scotland, save only the Scandinavian jarldoms of Caithness, Sutherland, and the Isles. Strathclyde rapidly adopted the tongue of its masters, and grew as English in language (though not in blood) as the Lothians themselves. Fife, in turn, was quickly Anglicised, as was also the whole region south of the Highland line. Thus a new and powerful kingdom arose in the North; and at the same time the cession of an English district to the Scottish kings had the curious result of thoroughly Anglicising two large and important Celtic regions, which had hitherto resisted every effort of the Northumbrian or West Saxon over-lords. There is no reason to believe, however, that this introduction of the English tongue and English manners was connected with any considerable immigration of Teutonic settlers into the Anglicised tracts. The population of Ayrshire, of Fife, of Perthshire, and of Aberdeen, still shows every sign of Celtic descent, alike in physique, in temperament, and in habit of thought. The change was, in all probability, exactly analogous to that which we ourselves have seen taking place in Wales, in Ireland, and in the Celtic north of Scotland at the present day.

1. See chapter xx.
2. It is impossible to avoid noticing the increased importance of semi-Celtic Britain under Dunstan's administration. He was himself at first an abbot of the old West Welsh monastery of Glastonbury: he promoted West countrymen to the principal posts in the kingdom: and he had Eadgar hallowed king at the ancient West Welsh royal city of Bath, married to a Devonshire lady, and buried at Glastonbury. Indeed, that monastery was under Dunstan what Westminster was under the later kings. Florence uses the strange expression that Eadgar was chosen "by the Anglo-Britons:" and the meeting with the Welsh and Scotch princes in the semi-Welsh town of Chester conveys a like implication.

* * * * *

CHAPTER XVI.

THE AUGUSTAN AGE AND THE LATER ANGLO-SAXON CIVILISATION.

The slight pause in the long course of Danish warfare which occurred during the vigorous administration of Dunstan, affords the best opportunity for considering the degree of civilisation reached by the English in the last age before the Norman Conquest. Our materials for such an estimate are partly to be found in existing buildings, manuscripts, pictures, ornaments, and other archæological remains, and partly in the documentary evidence of the chronicles and charters, and more especially of the great survey undertaken by the Conqueror's commissioners, and known as Domesday Book. From these sources we are enabled to gain a fairly complete view of the Anglo-Saxon culture in the period immediately preceding the immense influx of Romance civilisation after the Conquest; and though some such Romance influence was already exerted by the Normanising tendencies of Eadward the Confessor, we may yet conveniently consider the whole subject here under the age of Eadgar and Æthelred. It is difficult, indeed, to trace any very great improvement in the arts of life between the days of Dunstan and the days of Harold.

In spite of constant wars and ravages from the northern pirates, there can be little doubt that England had been slowly advancing in material civilisation ever since the introduction of Christianity. The heathen intermixture in the North and the Midlands had retarded the advance but had not completely checked it; while in Wessex and the South the intercourse with the continent and the consequent growth in culture had been steadily increasing. Æthelwulf of Wessex married a daughter of Karl the Bald; Ælfred gave his daughter to a count of Flanders; and Eadward's princesses were married respectively to the emperor, to the king of France, and to the king of Provence. Such alliances show a considerable degree of intercourse between Wessex and the Roman world; and the relics of material civilisation fully bear out the inference. The Institutes of the city of London mention traders from Brabant, Liège, Rouen, Ponthieu, France (in the restricted sense), and the Empire; but these came "in their own vessels." England, which now has in her hands the carrying trade of the world, was still dependent for her own supply on foreign bottoms. We know also that officers were appointed to collect tolls from foreign merchants at Canterbury, Dover, Arundel, and many other towns; and London and Bristol certainly traded on their own account with the Continent.

As a whole, however, England still remained a purely agricultural country to the very end of the Anglo-Saxon period. It had but little foreign trade, and what little existed was chiefly confined to imports of articles of luxury (wine, silk, spices, and artistic works) for the wealthier nobles, and of ecclesiastical requisites, such as pictures, incense, relics, vestments, and like southern products for the churches and monasteries. The exports seem mainly to have consisted of slaves and wool, though hides may possibly have been sent out of the country, and a little of the famous English gold-work and embroidery was perhaps sold abroad in return for the few imported luxuries. But taking the country at a glance, we must still picture it to ourselves as composed almost entirely of separate agricultural manors, each now owned by a considerable landowner, and tilled mainly by his churls, whose position had sunk during the Danish wars to that of semi-servile tenants, owing customary rents of labour to their superiors. War had told against the independence of the lesser freemen, who found themselves compelled to choose themselves protectors among the higher born classes, till at last the theory became general that every man must have a lord. The noble himself lived upon his manor, accepted service from his churls in tilling his own homestead, and allowed them lands in return in the outlying portions of his estates. His sources of income were two only: first, the agricultural produce of his lands, thus tilled for him by free labour and by the hands of his serfs; and secondly, the breeding of slaves, shipped from the ports of London and Bristol for the markets of the south. The artisans depended wholly upon their lord, being often serfs, or else churls holding on service-tenure. The mass of England consisted of such manors, still largely interspersed with woodland, each with the wooden hall of its lord occupying the centre of the homestead, and with the huts of the churls and serfs among the hays and valleys of the outskirts. The butter and cheese, bread and bacon, were made at home; the corn was ground in the quern; the beer was brewed and the honey collected by the family. The spinner and weaver, the shoemaker, smith, and carpenter, were all parts of the household. Thus every manor was wholly self-sufficing and self-sustaining, and towns were rendered almost unnecessary.

Forests and heaths still also covered about half the surface. These were now the hunting-grounds of the kings and nobles, while in the leys, hursts, and dens, small groups of huts gave shelter to the swineherds and woodwards who had charge of their lord's property in the woodlands. The great tree-covered region of Selwood still divided Wessex into two halves; the forest of the Chilterns still spread close to the walls of London; the Peakland was still overgrown by an inaccessible thicket; and the long central ridge between Yorkshire and Scotland was still shadowed by primæval oaks, pinewoods, and beeches. Agriculture continued to be confined to the alluvial bottoms, and had nowhere as yet invaded the uplands, or even the stiffer and drier lowland regions, such as the Weald of Kent or the forests of Arden and Elmet.

Only two elements broke the monotony of these self-sufficing agricultural communities. Those elements were the monasteries and the towns.

A large part of the soil of England was owned by the monks. They now possessed considerable buildings, with stone churches of some pretensions, in which service was conducted with pomp and impressiveness. The tiny chapel of St. Lawrence, at Bradford-on-Avon, forms the best example of this primitive Romanesque architecture now surviving in England. Around the monasteries stretched their well-tilled lands, mostly reclaimed from fen or forest, and probably more scientifically cultivated than those of the neighbouring manors. Most of the monks were skilled in civilised handicrafts, introduced from the more cultivated continent. They were excellent ecclesiastical metalworkers; many of them were architects, who built in rude imitation of Romanesque models; and others were designers or illuminators of manuscripts. The books and charters of this age are delicately and minutely wrought out, though not with all the artistic elaboration of later mediæval work. The art of painting (almost always in miniature) was considerably advanced, the figures being well drawn, in rather stiff but not unlifelike attitudes, though perspective is very imperfectly understood, and hardly ever attempted. Later Anglo-Saxon architecture, such as that of Eadward's magnificent abbey church at Westminster (afterwards destroyed by Henry III. to make way for his own building), was not inferior to continental workmanship. All the arts practised in the abbeys were of direct Roman origin, and most of the words relating to them are immediately derived from the Latin. This is the case even with terms relating to such common objects as *candle*, *pen*, *wine*, and *oil*. Names of weights, measures, coins, and other exact quantitative ideas are also derived from Roman sources. Carpenters, smiths, bakers, tanners, and millers, were usually attached to the abbeys. Thus, in many cases, as at Glastonbury, Peterborough, Ripon, Beverley, and Bury St. Edmunds, the monastery grew into the nucleus of a considerable town, though the development of such towns is more marked after than before the Norman Conquest. As a whole, it was by means of the monasteries, and especially of their constant interchange of inmates with the continent, that England mainly kept up the touch with the southern civilisation. There alone was Latin, the universal medium of continental intercommunication, taught and spoken. There alone were books written, preserved, and read. Through the Church alone was an organisation kept up in direct communication with the central civilising agencies of Italy and the south. And while the Church and the monasteries thus preserved the connection with the continent, they also formed schools of culture and of industrial arts for the country itself. At the abbeys bells were cast, glass manufactured, buildings designed, gold and silver ornaments wrought, jewels enamelled, and unskilled labour organised by the most trained intelligence of the land. They thus remained as they had begun, homes and retreats for those exceptional minds which were capable of carrying on the arts and the knowledge of a dying civilisation across the gulf of predatory barbarism which separates the artificial culture of Rome from the industrial culture of modern Europe.

The towns were few and relatively unimportant, built entirely of wood (except the churches), and very liable to be burnt down on the least excuse. In considering them we must dismiss from our minds the ideas derived from our own great and complex organisation, and bring ourselves mentally into the attitude of a simple agricultural people, requiring little beyond what was produced on each man's own farm or petty holding. Such people are mainly fed from their own corn and meat, mainly clad from their own homespun wool and linen. A little specialisation of function, however, already existed. Salt was procured from the wyches or pans of the coast, and also from the inland wyches or brine wells of Cheshire and the midland counties. Such names as Nantwich, Middlewych, Bromwich, and Droitwich, still preserve the memory of these early saltworks. Iron was mined in the Forest of Dean, around Alcester, and in the Somersetshire district. The city of Gloucester had six smiths' forges in the days of Eadward the Confessor, and paid its tax to the king in iron rods. Lead was found in Derbyshire, and was largely employed for roofing churches. Cloth-weaving was specially carried on at Stamford; but as a rule it is probable that every district supplied its own clothing. English merchants attended the great fair at St. Denys, in France, much as those of Central Asia now attend the fair at Kandahar; and madder seems to have been bought there for dyeing cloth. In Kent, Sussex, and East Anglia, herring fisheries already produced considerable results. With these few exceptions, all the towns were apparently mere local centres of exchange for produce, and small manufactured wares, like the larger villages or bazaars of India in our own time. Nevertheless, there was a distinct advance towards urban life in the later Anglo-Saxon period. Bæda mentions very few towns, and most of those were waste. By the date of the Conquest there were many, and their functions were such as befitted a more diversified national life. Communications had become far greater; and arts or trade had now to some extent specialised themselves in special places.

A list of the chief early English towns may possibly seem to give too much importance to these very minor elements of English life; yet one may, perhaps, be appended with due precaution against misapprehension.

The capital, if any place deserved to be so called under the perambulating early English dynasty, was Winchester (Wintan-ceaster), with its old and new minsters, containing the tombs of the West-Saxon kings. It possessed a large number of craftsmen, doubtless dependant ultimately upon the court; and it was relatively a place of far greater importance than at any later date.

The chief ports were London (Lundenbyrig), situated at the head of tidal navigation on the Thames; and Bristol (Bricgestow) and Gloucester (Gleawan-ceaster), similarly placed on the Avon and Severn. These towns were convenient for early shipping because of their tidal position, at an age when artificial harbours were unknown; They were the seat of the export traffic in slaves and the import traffic in continental goods. Before Ælfred's reign the carrying trade by sea seems to have been in the hands of the Frisian skippers and slave-dealers, who stood to the English in the same relation as the Arabs now stand to the East African and Central African negroes; but after the increased attention paid to shipbuilding during the struggle with the Danes, English vessels began to engage in trade on their own account. London must already have been the largest and richest town in the kingdom. Even in Bæda's time it was "the mart of many nations, resorting to it by sea and land." It seems, indeed, to have been a sort of merchant commonwealth, governed by its own port reeve, and it made its own dooms, which have been preserved to the present day. From the Roman time onward, the position of London as a great free commercial town was probably uninterrupted.

York (Eoforwic), the capital of the North, had its own archbishop and its Danish internal organisation. It seems to have been always an important and considerable town, and it doubtless possessed the same large body of handicraftsmen as Winchester. During the doubtful period of Danish and English struggles, the archbishop apparently exercised quasi-royal authority over the English burghers themselves.

Among the cathedral towns the most important were Canterbury (Cant-wara-byrig), the old capital of Kent and metropolis of all England, which seems to have contained a relatively large trading population; Dorchester, in Oxfordshire, first the royal city of the West Saxons, and afterwards the seat of the exiled bishopric of Lincoln; Rochester (Hrofes-ceaster), the old capital of the West Kentings, and seat of their bishop: and Worcester (Wigorna-ceaster), the chief town of the Huiccii. Of the monastic towns the chief were Peterborough (Burh), Ely (Elig), and Glastonbury (Glæstingabyrig). Bath, Amesbury, Colchester, Lincoln, Chester, and other towns of Roman origin were also important. Exeter, the old capital of the West Welsh, situated at the tidal head of the Exe, had considerable trade. Oxford was a place of traffic and a fortified town. Hastings, Dover, and the other south-coast ports had some communications with France. The only other places of any note were Chippenham, Bensington, and Aylesbury; Northampton and Southampton; Bamborough; the fortified posts built by Eadward and Æthelflæd; and the Danish boroughs of Bedford, Derby, Leicester, Stamford, Nottingham, and Huntingdon. The Witena-gemots and the synods took place in any town, irrespective of size, according to royal convenience. But as early as the days of Cnut, London was beginning to be felt as the real centre of national life: and Eadward the Confessor, by founding Westminster Abbey, made it practically the home of the kings. The Conqueror "wore his crown on Eastertide at Winchester; on Pentecost at Westminster; and on Midwinter at Gloucester:" which probably marks the relative position of the three towns as the chief places in the old West Saxon realm at least. Under Æthelstan, London had eight moneyers or mint-masters, while Winchester had only six, and Canterbury seven.

As regards the arts and traffic in the towns, they were chiefly carried on by guilds, which had their origin, as Dr. Brentano has shown with great probability, in separate families, who combined to keep up their own trade secrets as a family affair. In time, however, the guilds grew into regular organisations, having their own code of rules and laws, many of which (as at Cambridge, Exeter, and Abbotsbury) we still possess. It is possible that the families of craftsmen may at first have been Romanised Welsh inhabitants of the cities; for all the older towns—London, Canterbury, York, Lincoln, and Rochester—were almost certainly inhabited without interruption from the Roman period onward. But in any case the guilds seem to have grown out of family compacts, and to have retained always the character of close corporations. There must have been considerable division of the various trades even before the Conquest, and each trade must have inhabited a separate quarter; for we find at Winchester, or elsewhere, in the reign of Æthelred, Fellmonger, Horsemonger, Fleshmonger, Shieldwright, Shoewright, Turner, and Salter Streets.

The exact amount of the population of England cannot be ascertained, even approximately; but we may obtain a rough approximation from the estimates based upon Domesday Book. It seems probable that at the end of the Conqueror's reign, England contained 1,800,000 souls. Allowing for the large number of persons introduced at the Conquest, and for the natural increase during the unusual peace in the reigns of Cnut, of Eadward the Confessor, and, above all, of William himself, we may guess that it could not have contained more than a million and a quarter in the days of Eadgar. London may have had a population of some 10,000; Winchester and York of 5,000 each; certainly that of York at the date of Domesday could not have exceeded 7,000 persons, and we know that it contained 1,800 houses in the time of Eadward the Confessor.

The organisation of the country continued on the lines of the old constitution. But the importance of the simple freeman had now quite died out, and the gemot was rather a meeting of the earls, bishops, abbots, and wealthy landholders, than a real assembly of the people. The sub-divisions of the kingdom were now pretty generally conterminous with the modern counties. In Wessex and the east the counties are either older kingdoms, like Kent, Sussex, and Essex; or else tribal divisions of the kingdom, like Dorset, Somerset, Norfolk, Suffolk, and Surrey. In Mercia, the recovered country is artificially mapped out round the chief Danish burgs, as in the case of Derbyshire, Nottinghamshire, Bedfordshire, Northamptonshire, and Leicestershire, where the county town usually occupies the centre of the arbitrary shire. In Northumbria it is divided into equally artificial counties by the rivers. Beneath the counties stood the older organisation of the hundred, and beneath that again the primitive unit of the township, known on its ecclesiastical side as the parish. In the reign of Eadgar, England seems to have contained about 3,000 parish churches.

* * * * *

CHAPTER XVII.

THE DECADENCE.

The death of Dunstan was the signal for the breaking down of the artificial kingdom which he had held together by the mere power of his solitary organising capacity. Æthelred, the son of Eadgar (who succeeded after the brief reign of his brother Eadward), lost hopelessly all hold over the Scandinavian north. At the same time, the wicking incursions, intermitted for nearly a century, once more recommenced with the same vigour as of old. Even before Dunstan's death, in 980, the pirates ravaged Southampton, killing most of the townsfolk; and they also pillaged Thanet, while another host overran Cheshire. In the succeeding year, "great harm was done in Devonshire and in Wales;" and a year later again, London was burnt and Portland ravaged. In 985, Æthelred, the Unready, as after ages called him, from his lack of *rede* or counsel, quarrelled with Ælfric, ealdormen of the Mercians, whom he drove over sea. The breach between Mercia and Wessex was thus widened, and as the Danish attacks continued without interruption the redeless king soon found himself comparatively isolated in his own paternal dominions. Northumbria, under its earl, Uhtred (one of the house of Bamborough), and the Five Burgs under their Danish leaders, acted almost independently of Wessex throughout the whole of Æthelred's reign. In 991 Sigeric, archbishop of Canterbury, advised that the Danes should be bought off by a payment of ten thousand pounds, an enormous sum; but it was raised somehow and duly paid. In 992, the command of a naval force, gathered from the merchant craft of the Thames, was entrusted to Ælfric, who had been recalled; and the Mercian leader went over on the eve of an engagement at London to the side of the enemy. Bamborough was stormed and captured with great booty, and the host sailed up Humber mouth. There they stood in the midst of the old Danish kingdom, and found the leading men of Northumbria and Lindsey by no means unfriendly to their invasion. In fact, the Danish north was now far more ready to welcome the kindred Scandinavian than the West Saxon stranger. Æthelred's realm practically shrank at once to the narrow limits of Kent and Wessex.

The Danes, however, were by no means content even with these successes. Olaf Tryggvesson, king of Norway, and Swegen Forkbeard,[1] king of Denmark, fell upon England. The era of mere plundering expeditions and of scattered colonisation had ceased; the era of political conquest had now begun. They had determined upon the complete subjugation of all England. In 994 Olaf and Swegen attacked London with 94 ships, but were put to flight by a gallant resistance of the townsmen, who did "more harm and evil than ever they weened that any burghers could do them." Thence the host sailed away to Essex, Kent, Sussex, and Hampshire, burning and slaying all along the coast as they went. Æthelred and his witan bought them off again, with the immense tribute of sixteen thousand pounds. The host accepted the terms, but settled down for the winter at Southampton—a sufficient indication of their intentions—within easy reach of Winchester itself; and there "they fed from all the West Saxons' land." Æthelred was alarmed, and sent to Olaf, who consented to meet him at Andover. There the king received him "with great worship," and gifted him with kinglike gifts, and sent him away with a promise never again to attack England. Olaf kept his word, and returned no more. But still Swegen remained, and went on pillaging Devonshire and Cornwall, wending into Tamar mouth as far as Lidford, where his men "burnt and slew all that they found." Thence they betook themselves to the Frome, and so up into Dorset, and again to Wight. In 999, on the eve of doomsday as men then thought, they sailed up Thames and Medway, and attacked Rochester. The men of Kent stoutly fought them, but, as usual, without assistance from other shires; and the Danes took horses, and rode over the land, almost ruining all the West Kentings. The king and his witan resolved to send against them a land fyrd and a ship fyrd or raw levy. But the spirit of the West Saxons was broken, and though the craft were gathered together, yet in the end, as the Chronicle plaintively puts it, "neither ship fyrd nor land fyrd wrought anything save toil for the folk, and the emboldening of their foes."

So, year after year, the endless invasion dragged on its course, and everywhere each shire of Wessex fought for itself against such enemies as happened to attack it. At last, in the year 1002, Æthelred once more bought off the fleet, this time with 24,000 pounds; and some of the Danes obtained leave to settle down in Wessex. But on St. Brice's day, the king treacherously gave orders that all Danes in the immediate English territory should be massacred. The West Saxons rose on the appointed night, and slew every one of them, including Gunhild, the sister of King Swegen, and a Christian convert. It was a foolhardy attempt. Swegen fell at once upon Wessex, and marched up and down the whole country, for two years. He burnt Wilton and Sarum, and then sailed round to Norwich, where Ulfkytel, of East Anglia, gave him "the hardest hand-play" that he had ever known in England. A year of famine intervened; but in 1006 Swegen returned again, harrying and burning Sandwich. All autumn the West Saxon fyrd waited for the enemy, but in the end "it came to naught more than it had oft erst done." The host took up quarters in Wight, marched across Hants and Berks to Reading, and burned Wallingford. Thence they returned with their booty to the fleet, by the very walls of the royal city. "There might the Winchester folk behold an insolent host and fearless wend past their gate to sea." The king himself had fled into Shropshire. The tone of utter despair with which the Chronicle narrates all these events is the best measure of the national degradation. "There was so muckle awe of the host," says the annalist, "that no man could think how man could drive them from this earth or hold this earth against them; for that they had cruelly marked each shire of Wessex with burning and with harrying." The English had sunk into hopeless misery, and were only waiting for a strong rule to rescue them from their misery.

The strong rule came at last. Thorkell, a Danish jarl, marched all through Wessex, and for three years more his host pillaged everywhere in the South. In 1011, they killed Ælfheah, the archbishop of Canterbury, at Greenwich. When the country was wholly weakened, Swegen turned southward once more, this time with all Northumbria and Mercia at his back. In 1013 he sailed round to Humber mouth, and thence up the Trent, to Gainsborough. "Then Earl Uhtred and all Northumbrians soon bowed to him, and all the folk in Lindsey; and sithence the folk of the Five Burgs, and shortly after, all the host by north of Watling-street; and men gave him hostages of each shire." Swegen at once led the united army into England, leaving his son Cnut in Denalagu with the ships and hostages. He marched to Oxford, which received him; then to the royal city of Winchester, which made no resistance. At London Æthelred was waiting; and for a time the town held out. So Swegen marched westward, and took Bath. There, the thegns of the Welsh-kin counties—Somerset, Dorset, Devon, and Cornwall—bowed to him and gave him hostages. "When he had thus fared, he went north to his ships, and all the folk held him then as full king." London itself gave way. Æthelred fled to Wight, and thence to Normandy. He had married Ymma, the daughter of Richard the Fearless; and he now took refuge with her brother, Richard the Good.

Next year Swegen died, and the West Saxon witan sent back for Æthelred. No lord was dearer to them, they said, than their lord by kin. But the host had already chosen Cnut; and the host had a stronger claim than the witan. For two years Æthelred carried on a desultory war with the intruders, and then died, leaving it undecided. His son Eadmund, nicknamed Ironside, continued the contest for a few months; but in the autumn of 1016 he died—poisoned, the English said, by Cnut—and Cnut succeeded to undisputed sway. He at once assumed Wessex as his own peculiar dominion, and the political history of the English ends for two centuries. Their social life went on, of course, as ever; but it was the life of a people in strict subjection to foreign rulers—

Danish, Norman, or Angevin. The story of the next twenty-five years at least belongs to the chronicles of Scandinavian Britain.

At the end of that time, however, there was a slight reaction. Cnut and his sons had bound the kingdom roughly into one; and the death of Harthacnut left an opportunity for the return of a descendant of Ælfred. But the English choice fell upon one who was practically a foreigner. Eadward, son of Æthelred by Ymma of Normandy, had lived in his mother's country during the greater part of his life. Recalled by Earl Godwine and the witan, he came back to England a Norman, rather than an Englishman. The administration remained really in the hands of Godwine himself, and of the Danish or Danicised aristocracy. But Mercia and Northumbria still stood apart from Wessex, and once procured the exile of Godwine himself. The great earl returned, however, and at his death passed on his power to his son Harold, a Danicised Englishman of great rough ability, such as suited the hard times on which he was cast. Harold employed the lifetime of Eadward, who was childless, in preparing for his own succession. The king died in 1066, and Harold was quietly chosen at once by the witan. He was the last Englishman who ever sat upon the throne of England.

The remaining story belongs chiefly to the annals of Norman Britain. Harold was assailed at once from either side. On the north, his brother Tostig, whom he had expelled from Northumbria, led against him his namesake, Harold Hardrada, king of Norway. On the south, William of Normandy, Eadward's cousin, claimed the right to present himself to the English electors. Eadward's death, in fact, had broken up the temporary status, and left England once more a prey to barbaric Scandinavians from Denmark, or civilised Scandinavians from Normandy. The English themselves had no organisation which could withstand either, and no national unity to promote such organisation in future. Harold of Norway came first, landing in the old Danish stronghold of Northumbria; and the English Harold hurried northward to meet him, with his little body of house-carls, aided by a large fyrd which he had hastily collected to use against William. At Stamford-bridge he overthrew the invaders with great slaughter, Harold Hardrada and Tostig being amongst the slain. Meanwhile, William had crossed to Pevensey, and was ravaging the coast. Harold hurried southward, and met him at Senlac, near Hastings. After a hard day's fight, the Normans were successful, and Harold fell. But even yet the English could not agree among themselves. In this crisis of the national fate, the local jealousies burnt up as fiercely as ever. While William was marching upon London, the witan were quarrelling and intriguing in the city over the succession. "Archbishop Ealdred and the townsmen of London would have Eadgar Child,"—a grandson of Eadmund Ironside—"for king, as was his right by kin." But Eadwine and Morkere, the representatives of the great Mercian family of Leofric, had hopes that they might turn William's invasion to their own good, and secure their independence in the north by allowing Wessex to fall unassisted into his hands. After much shuffling, Eadgar was at last chosen for king. "But as it ever should have been the forwarder, so was it ever, from day to day, slower and worse." No resistance was organised. In the midst of all this turmoil, the Peterborough Chronicler is engaged in narrating the petty affairs of his own abbey, and the question which arose through the application made to Eadgar for his consent to the appointment of an abbot. In such a spirit did the English meet an invasion from the stoutest and best organised soldiery in Europe. William marched on without let or hindrance, and on his way, the Lady—the Confessor's widow—surrendered the royal city of Winchester into his hands. The duke reached the Thames, burnt Southwark, and then made a détour to cross the river at Wallingford, whence he proceeded into Hertfordshire, thus cutting off Eadwine and Morkere in London from their earldoms. The Mercian and Northumbrian leaders being determined to hold their own at all hazards, retreated northward; and the English resistance crumbled into pieces. Eadgar, the rival king, with Ealdred, the archbishop, and all the chief men of London, came out to meet William, and "bowed to him for need." The Chronicler can only say that it was very foolish they had not done so before. A people so helpless, so utterly anarchic, so incapable of united action, deserved to undergo a severe training from the hard taskmasters of Romance civilisation. The nation remained, but it remained as a conquered race, to be drilled in the stern school of the conquerors. For awhile, it is true, William governed England like an English king; but the constant rebellion and faithlessness of his new subjects drove him soon to severer measures; and the great insurrection of 1068, with its results, put the whole country at his feet in a very different sense from the battle of Senlac. For a hundred and fifty years, the English people remained a mere race of chapmen and serfs; and the English language died down meanwhile into a servile dialect. When the native stock emerges again into the full light of history, by the absorption of the Norman conquerors in the reign of John, it reappears with all the super-added culture and organisation of the Romance nationalities. The Conquest was an inevitable step in the work of severing England from the barbarous North, and binding it once more in bonds of union with the civilised South. It was the necessary undoing of the Danish conquest; more still, it was an inevitable step in the process whereby England itself was to begin its unified existence by the final breaking down of the barriers which divided Wessex from Mercia, and Mercia from Northumbria.

1. See Mr. York-Powell's "Scandinavian Britain."

* * * * *

CHAPTER XVIII.

THE ANGLO-SAXON LANGUAGE.

A description of Anglo-Saxon Britain, however brief, would not be complete without some account of the English language in its earliest and purest form. But it would be impossible within reasonable limits to give anything more than a short general statement of the relation which the old English tongue bears to the kindred Teutonic dialects, and of the main differences which mark it off from our modern simplified and modified speech. All that can be attempted here is such a broad outline as may enable the general reader to grasp the true connexion between modern English and so-called Anglo-Saxon, on the one hand, as well as between Anglo-Saxon itself and the parent Teutonic language on the other. Any full investigation of grammatical or etymological details would be beyond the scope of this little volume.

The tongue spoken by the English and Saxons at the period of their invasion of Britain was an almost unmixed Low Dutch dialect. Originally derived, of course, from the primitive Aryan language, it had already undergone those changes which are summed up in what is known as Grimm's Law. The principal consonants in the old Aryan tongue had been regularly and slightly altered in certain directions; and these alterations have been carried still further in the allied High German language. Thus the original word for *father*, which closely resembled the Latin *pater*, becomes in early English or Anglo-Saxon *fæder*, and in modern High German *vater*. So, again, among the numerals, our *two*, in early English *twa*, answers to Latin *duo* and modern

High German *zwei*; while our *three*, in old English *threo*, answers to Latin *tres*, and modern High German *drei*. So far as these permutations are concerned, Sanscrit, Greek, and Latin may be regarded as most nearly resembling the primitive Aryan speech, and with them the Celtic dialects mainly agree. From these, the English varies one degree, the High German two. The following table represents the nature of such changes approximately for these three groups of languages:—

Greek, Sanscrit, Latin, Celtic	p.	b.	f.	t.	d.	th.	k.	g.	ch.
Gothic, English, Low Dutch	f.	p.	b.	th.	t.	d.	ch.	k.	g.
High German		b.	f.	p.	d.	th.	t.	g.	ch.	k.

In practice, several modifications arise; for example, the law is only true for old High German, and that only approximately, but its general truth may be accepted as governing most individual cases.

Judged by this standard, English forms a dialect of the Low Dutch branch of the Aryan language, together with Frisian, modern Dutch, and the Scandinavian tongues. Within the group thus restricted its affinities are closest with Frisian and old Dutch, less close with Icelandic and Danish. While the English still lived on the shores of the Baltic, it is probable that their language was perfectly intelligible to the ancestors of the people who now inhabit Holland, and who then spoke very slightly different local dialects. In other words, a single Low Dutch speech then apparently prevailed from the mouth of the Elbe to that of the Scheldt, with small local variations; and from this speech the Anglo-Saxon and the modern English have developed in one direction, while the Dutch has developed in another, the Frisian dialect long remaining intermediate between them. Scandinavian ceased, perhaps, to be intelligible to Englishmen at an earlier date, the old Icelandic being already marked off from Anglo-Saxon by strong peculiarities, while modern Danish differs even more widely from the spoken English of the present day.

The relation of Anglo-Saxon to modern English is that of direct parentage, it might almost be said of absolute identity. The language of

Beowulf and of Ælfred is not, as many people still imagine, a different language from our own; it is simply English in its earliest and most unmixed form. What we commonly call Anglo-Saxon, indeed, is more English than what we commonly call English at the present day. The first is truly English, not only in its structure and grammar, but also in the whole of its vocabulary: the second, though also truly English in its structure and grammar, contains a large number of Latin, Greek, and Romance elements in its vocabulary. Nevertheless, no break separates us from the original Low Dutch tongue spoken in the marsh lands of Sleswick. The English of *Beowulf* grows slowly into the English of Ælfred, into the English of Chaucer, into the English of Shakespeare and Milton, and into the English of Macaulay and Tennyson.

Old words drop out from time to time, old grammatical forms die away or become obliterated, new names and verbs are borrowed, first from the Norman-French at the Conquest, then from the classical Greek and Latin at the Renaissance; but the continuity of the language remains unbroken, and its substance is still essentially the same as at the beginning. The Cornish, the Irish, and to some extent the Welsh, have left off speaking their native tongues, and adopted the language of the dominant Teuton; but there never was a time when Englishmen left off speaking Anglo-Saxon and took to English, Norman-French, or any other form of speech whatsoever.

An illustration may serve to render clearer this fundamental and important distinction. If at the present day a body of Englishmen were to settle in China, they might learn and use the Chinese names for many native plants, animals, and manufactured articles; but however many of such words they adopted into their vocabulary, their language would still remain essentially English. A visitor from England would have to learn a number of unfamiliar words, but he would not have to learn a new language. If, on the other hand, a body of Frenchmen were to settle in a neighbouring Chinese province, and to adopt exactly the same Chinese words, their language would still remain essentially French. The dialects of the two settlements would contain many words in common, but neither of them would be a Chinese dialect on that account. Just so, English since the Norman Conquest has grafted many foreign words upon the native stock; but it still remains at bottom the same language as in the days of Eadgar.

Nevertheless, Anglo-Saxon differs so far in externals from modern English, that it is now necessary to learn it systematically with grammar and dictionary, in somewhat the same manner as one would learn a foreign tongue. Most of the words, indeed, are more or less familiar, at least so far as their roots are concerned; but the inflexions of the nouns and verbs are far more complicated than those now in use: and many obsolete forms occur even in the vocabulary. On the other hand the idioms closely resemble those still in use; and even where a root has now dropped out of use, its meaning is often immediately suggested by the cognate High German word, or by some archaic form preserved for us in Chaucer, Shakespeare, or Milton, as well as by occasional survival in the Lowland Scotch and other local dialects.

English in its early form was an inflexional language; that is to say, the mutual relations of nouns and of verbs were chiefly expressed, not by means of particles, such as *of*, *to*, *by*, and so forth, but by means of modifications either in the termination or in the body of the root itself. The nouns were declined much as in Greek and Latin; the verbs were conjugated in somewhat the same way as in modern French. Every noun had gender expressed in its form.

The following examples will give a sufficient idea of the commoner forms of declension in the classical West Saxon of the time of Ælfred. The pronunciation has already been briefly explained in the preface.

	SING.		PLUR.
(1.) *Nom.*	stan (*a stone*).	*Nom.*	stanas.
Gen.	stanes.	Gen.	stana.
Dat.	stane.	Dat.	stanum.
Acc.	stan.	Acc.	stanas.

This is the commonest declension for masculine nouns, and it has fixed the normal plural for the modern English.

	SING.		PLUR.
(2.) *Nom.*	fot (*a foot*).	Nom.	fet.
Gen.	fotes.	Gen.	fota.
Dat.	fet.	Dat.	fotum.
Acc.	fot.	Acc.	fet.

Hence our modified plurals, such as *feet*, *teeth*, and *men*.

	SING.		PLUR.
(3.) *Nom.*	wudu (*a wood*).	*Nom.*	wuda.
Gen.	wuda.	Gen.	wuda.
Dat.	wuda.	Dat.	wudum.
Acc.	wudu.	Acc.	wuda.

All these are for masculine nouns.
The commonest feminine declension is as follows:—

	SING.		PLUR.
(4.) *Nom.*	gifu (*a gift*).	*Nom.*	gifa.
Gen.	gife.	Gen.	gifena.
Dat.	gife.	Dat.	gifum.
Acc.	gife.	Acc.	gifa.

Less frequent is the modified form:

	SING.		PLUR.
(5.) *Nom.*	boc (*a book*).	*Nom.*	bec.
Gen.	bec.	Gen.	boca.
Dat.	bec.	Dat.	bocum.
Acc.	boc.	Acc.	bec.

Of neuters there are two principal declensions. The first has the plural in *u*; the second leaves it unchanged.

	SING.		PLUR.
(6.) *Nom.*	scip (*a ship*).	*Nom.*	scipu.
Gen.	scipes.	Gen.	scipa.
Dat.	scipe.	Dat.	scipum.
Acc.	scip.	Acc.	scipu.

	SING.		PLUR.
(7.) *Nom.*	hus (*a house*).	*Nom.*	hus.
Gen.	huses.	Gen.	husa.
Dat.	huse.	Dat.	husum.
Acc.	hus.	Acc.	hus.

Hence our "collective" plurals, such as *fish*, *deer*, *sheep*, and *trout*.

There is also a weak declension, much the same for all three genders, of which the masculine form runs as follows:—

	SING.		PLUR.
Nom.	guma (*a man*).	*Nom.*	guman.
Gen.	guman.	Gen.	gumena.
Dat.	guman.	Dat.	guman.
Acc.	guman.	Acc.	guman.

Adjectives are declined throughout, as in Latin, through all the cases (including an instrumental), numbers, and genders. The demonstrative pronoun or definite article *se* (the) may stand as an example.

SING.

	Masc.	Fem.	Neut.
Nom.	se,	seo,	thæt.
Gen.	thæs,	thære,	thæs.

Dat.	tham,	thære,	tham.
Acc.	thone,	tha,	thæt.
Inst.	thy,	thære,	thy.

PLUR.

Masc. Fem. Neut.

Nom.	tha.
Gen.	thara.
Dat.	tham.
Acc.	tha.
Inst.	—

Verbs are conjugated about as fully as in Latin. There are two principal forms: strong verbs, which form their preterite by vowel modification, as *binde*, pret. *band*; and weak verbs, which form it by the addition of *ode* or *de* to the root, as *lufige*, pret. *lufode*; *hire*, pret. *hirde*. The present and preterite of the first form are as follows:—

		IND.	SUBJ.
Pres. sing.	1.	binde.	binde.
	2.	bindest.	binde.
	3.	bindeth.	binde.
plur.	1, 2, 3.	bindath.	binden.
Pret. sing.	1.	band.	bunde.
	2.	bunde.	bunde.
	3.	band.	bunde.
plur.	1, 2, 3.	bundon	bunden.

Both the grammatical forms and still more the orthography vary much from time to time, from place to place, and even from writer to writer. The forms used in this work are for the most part those employed by West Saxons in the age of Ælfred.

A few examples of the language as written at three periods will enable the reader to form some idea of its relation to the existing type. The first passage cited is from King Ælfred's translation of Orosius; but it consists of the opening lines of a paragraph inserted by the king himself from his own materials, and so affords an excellent illustration of his style in original English prose. The reader is recommended to compare it word for word with the parallel slightly modernised version, bearing in mind the inflexional terminations.

Ohthere sæde his hlaforde, Ælfrede cyninge, thæt he ealra Northmonna northmest bude. He cwæth thæt he bude on thæm lande northweardum with tha West-sæ. He sæde theah thæt thæt land sie swithe lang north thonan; ac hit is eall weste, buton on feawum stowum styccemælum wiciath Finnas, on huntothe on wintra, and on sumera on fiscathe be thære sæ. He sæde thæt he æt sumum cirre wolde fandian hu longe thæt land northryhte læge, oththe hwæther ænig monn be northan thæm westenne bude. Tha for he northryhte be thæm lande: let him ealne weg thæt weste land on thæt steorbord, and tha wid-sæ on thæt bæcbord thrie dagas. Tha wæs he swa feor north swa tha hwæl-huntan firrest farath.

Othhere said [to] his lord, Ælfred king, that he of all Northmen northmost abode. He quoth that he abode on the land northward against the West Sea. He said, though, that that land was [or extended] much north thence; eke it is all waste, but [except that] on few stows [in a few places] piecemeal dwelleth Finns, on hunting on winter, and on summer on fishing by the sea. He said that he at some time [on one occasion] would seek how long that land lay northright [due north], or whether any man by north of the waste abode. Then fore [fared] he northright, by the land: left all the way that waste land on the starboard of him, and the wide sea on the backboard [port, French *babord*] three days. Then was he so far north as the whale-hunters furthest fareth.

146

In this passage it is easy to see that the variations which make it into modern English are for the most part of a very simple kind. Some of the words are absolutely identical, as *his, on, he, and, land,* or *north*. Others, though differences of spelling mask the likeness, are practically the same, as *sæ, sæde, cwæth, thæt, lang,* for which we now write *sea, said, quoth, that, long*. A few have undergone contraction or alteration, as *hlaford,* now *lord, cyning,* now *king,* and *steorbord,* now *starboard*. *Stow,* a place, is now obsolete, except in local names; *styccemælum,* stickmeal, has been Normanised into *piecemeal*. In other cases new terminations have been substituted for old ones; *huntath* and *fiscath* are now replaced by *hunting* and *fishing;* while *hunta* has been superseded by *hunter*. Only six words in the passage have died out wholly: *buan,* to abide (*bude*); *swithe,* very; *wician,* to dwell; *cirr,* an occasion; *fandian,* to enquire (connected with *find*); and *bæcbord,* port, which still survives in French from Norman sources. *Dæg,* day, and *ænig,* any, show how existing English has softened the final *g* into a *y*. But the main difference which separates the modern passage from its ancient prototype is the consistent dropping of the grammatical inflexions in *hlaforde, Ælfrede, ealra, feawum,* and *fandian,* where we now say, *to his lord, of all, in few,* and *to enquire*.

The next passage, from the old English epic of Beowulf, shows the language in another aspect. Here, as in all poetry, archaic forms abound, and the syntax is intentionally involved. It is written in the old alliterative rhythm, described in the next chapter:—

Beowulf mathelode   bearn Ecgtheowes;
Hwæt! we the thas sæ-lac   sunu Healfdenes
Leod Scyldinga   lustum brohton,
Tires to tacne,   the thu her to-locast.
Ic thæt un-softe   ealdre gedigde
Wigge under wætere,   weore genethde
Earfothlice;   æt rihte wæs
Guth getwæfed   nymthe mec god scylde.

Beowulf spake,	the son of Ecgtheow:
See! We to thee this sea-gift,	son of Healfdene,
Prince of the Scyldings,	joyfully have brought,
For a token of glory,	that thou here lookest on.
That I unsoftly,	gloriously accomplished,
In war under water:	the work I dared,
With much labour:	rightly was
The battle divided,	but that a god shielded me.

Or, to translate more prosaically:—

"Beowulf, the son of Ecgtheow, addressed the meeting. See, son of Healfdene, Prince of the Scyldings; we have joyfully brought thee this gift from the sea which thou beholdest, for a proof of our valour. I obtained it with difficulty, gloriously, fighting beneath the waves: I dared the task with great toil. Evenly was the battle decreed, but that a god afforded me his protection."

In this short passage, many of the words are now obsolete: for example, *mathelian*, to address an assembly (*concionari*); *lac*, a gift; *wig*, war; *guth*, battle; and *leod*, a prince. *Ge-digde*, *ge-nethde*, and *ge-twæfed* have the now obsolete particle *ge-*, which bears much the same sense as in High German. On the other hand, *bearn*, a bairn; *sunu*, a son; *sæ*, sea; *tacen*, a token; *wæter*, water; and *weorc*, work, still survive: as do the verbs *to bring*, *to look*, and *to shield*. *Lust*, pleasure, whence *lustum*, joyfully, has now restricted its meaning in modern English, but retains its original sense in High German.

A few lines from the "Chronicle" under the year 1137, during the reign of Stephen, will give an example of Anglo-Saxon in its later and corrupt form, caught in the act of passing into Chaucerian English:—

This gære for the King Stephan ofer sæ to Normandi; and ther wes under fangen, forthi thæt hi wenden thæt he sculde ben alsuic alse the eom wæs, and for he hadde get his tresor; ac he todeld it and scatered sotlice. Micel hadde Henri king gadered gold and sylver, and na god ne dide men for his saule tharof. Tha the King Stephan to Englaland com, tha macod he his gadering æt Oxeneford, and thar he nam the biscop Roger of Sereberi, and Alexander biscop of Lincoln, and the Canceler Roger, hise neves, and dide ælle in prisun, til hi iafen up hire castles.

This year fared the King Stephen over sea to Normandy; and there he was accepted [received as duke] because that they weened that he should be just as his uncle was, and because he had got his treasure: but he to-dealt [distributed] and scattered it sot-like [foolishly]. Muckle had King Henry gathered of gold and silver; and man did no good for his soul thereof. When that King Stephan was come to England, then maked he his gathering at Oxford, and there he took the bishop Roger of Salisbury, and Alexander, bishop of Lincoln, and the Chancellor Roger, his nephew, and did them all in prison [put them in prison] till they gave up their castles.

The following passage from Ælfric's Life of King Oswold, in the best period of early English prose, may perhaps be intelligible to modern readers by the aid of a few explanatory notes only. *Mid* means *with*; while *with* itself still bears only the meaning of *against*:—

"Æfter tham the Augustinus to Englalande becom, wæs sum æthele cyning, Oswold ge-haten [*hight* or *called*], on North-hymbra-lande, ge-lyfed swithe on God. Se ferde [went] on his iugothe [youth] fram his freondum and magum [relations] to Scotlande on sæ, and thær sona wearth ge-fullod [baptised], and his ge-feran [companions] samod the mid him sithedon [journeyed]. Betwux tham wearth of-slagen [off-slain] Eadwine his eam [uncle], North-hymbra cyning, on Crist ge-lyfed, fram Brytta cyninge, Ceadwalla ge-ciged [called, named], and twegen his æfter-gengan binnan twam gearum [years]; and se Ceadwalla sloh and to sceame tucode tha North-hymbran leode [people] æfter heora hlafordes fylle, oth thæt [until] Oswold se eadiga his yfelnysse adwæscte [extinguished]. Oswold him com to, and him cenlice [boldly] with feaht mid lytlum werode [troop], ac his geleafa [belief] hine ge-trymde [encouraged], and Crist him ge-fylste [helped] to his feonda [fiends, enemies] slege."

It will be noticed in every case that the syntactical arrangement of the words in the sentences follows as a whole the rule that the governed word precedes the governing, as in Latin or High German, not *vice versa*, as in modern English.

A brief list will show the principal modifications undergone by nouns in the process of modernisation. *Stan*, stone; *snaw*, snow; *ban*, bone. *Cræft*, craft; *stæf*, staff; *bæc*, back. *Weg*, way; *dæg*, day; *nægel*, nail; *fugol*, fowl. *Gear*, year; *geong*, young. *Finger*, finger; *winter*, winter; *ford*, ford. *Æfen*, even; *morgen*, morn. *Monath*, month; *heofon*, heaven; *heafod*, head. *Fot*, foot; *toth*, tooth; *boc*, book; *freond*, friend. *Modor*, mother; *fæder*, father; *dohtor*, daughter. *Sunu*, son; *wudu*, wood; *caru*, care; *denu*, dene (valley). *Scip*, ship; *cild*, child; *ceorl*, churl; *cynn*, kin; *ceald*, cold. Wherever a word has not become wholly obsolete, or assumed a new termination, (*e.g.*, *gifu*, gift; *morgen*, morn-ing), it usually follows one or other of these analogies.

The changes which the English language, as a whole, has undergone in passing from its earlier to its later form, may best be considered under the two heads of form and matter.

As regards form or structure, the language has been simplified in three separate ways. First, the nouns and adjectives have for the most part lost their inflexions, at least so far as the cases are concerned. Secondly, the nouns have also lost their gender. And thirdly, the verbs have been simplified in conjugation, weak preterites being often substituted for strong ones, and differential terminations largely lost. On the other hand, the plural of nouns is still distinguished from the singular by its termination in *s*, which is derived from the first declension of Anglo-Saxon nouns, not as is often asserted, from the Norman-French usage. In other words, all plurals have been assimilated to this the commonest model; just as in French they have been assimilated to the final *s* of the third declension in Latin. A few plurals of the other types still survive, such as *men, geese, mice, sheep, deer, oxen, children* and (dialectically) *peasen*. To make up for this loss of inflexions, the language now employs a larger number of particles, and to some extent, of auxiliaries. Instead of *wines*, we now say *of a friend*; instead of *wine*, we now say *to a friend*; and instead of *winum*, we now say *to friends*. English, in short, has almost ceased to be inflexional and has become analytic.

As regards matter or vocabulary, the language has lost in certain directions, and gained in others. It has lost many old Teutonic roots, such as *wig*, war; *rice*, kingdom; *tungol*, light; with their derivatives, *wigend*, warrior; *rixian*, to rule; *tungol-witega*, astrologer; and so forth. The relative number of such losses to the survivals may be roughly gauged from the passages quoted above. On the other hand, the language has gained by the incorporation of many Romance words, shortly after the Norman Conquest, such as *place, voice, judge, war*, and *royal*. Some of these have entirely superseded native old English words. Thus the Norman-French *uncle, aunt, cousin, nephew*, and *niece*, have wholly ousted their Anglo-Saxon equivalents. In other instances the Romance words have enriched the language with symbols for really new ideas. This is still more strikingly the case with the direct importations from the classical Greek and Latin which began at the period of the Renaissance. Such words usually refer either to abstract conceptions for which the English language had no suitable expression, or to the accurate terminology of the advanced sciences. In every-day conversation our vocabulary is almost entirely English; in speaking or writing upon philosophical or scientific subjects it is largely intermixed with Romance and Græco-Latin elements. On the whole, though it is to be regretted that many strong, vigorous or poetical old Teutonic roots should have been allowed to fall into disuse, it may safely be asserted that our gains have far more than outbalanced our losses in this respect.

It must never be forgotten, however, that the whole framework of our language still remains, in every case, purely English—that is to say, Anglo-Saxon or Low Dutch—however many foreign elements may happen to enter into its vocabulary. We can frame many sentences without using one word of Romance or classical origin: we cannot frame a single sentence without using words of English origin. The Authorised Version of the Bible, "The Pilgrim's Progress," and such poems as Tennyson's "Dora," consist almost entirely of Teutonic elements. Even when the vocabulary is largely classical, as in Johnson's "Rasselas" and some parts of "Paradise Lost," the grammatical structure, the prepositions, the pronouns, the auxiliary verbs, and the connecting particles, are all necessarily and purely English. Two examples will suffice to make this principle perfectly clear. In the first, which is the most familiar quotation from Shakespeare, all the words of foreign origin have been printed in italics:—

> To be, or not to be,—that is the *question*:
> Whether 'tis *nobler* in the mind to suffer
> The slings and arrows of *outrageous fortune*;
> Or to take arms against a *sea* of *troubles*,
> And, by *opposing*, end them? To die,—to sleep,—
> No more; and, by a sleep, to say we end
> The heart-ache, and the thousand *natural* shocks
> That flesh is heir to,—'tis a *consummation*
> *Devoutly* to be wished. To die,—to sleep;—
> To sleep! *perchance* to dream: ay, there's the rub
> For in that sleep of death what dreams may come,
> When we have shuffled off this *mortal coil*,
> Must give us *pause*: there's the *respect*

That makes calamity of so long life;
For who would bear the whips and scorns of time,
The oppressor's wrong, the proud man's contumely,
The pangs of despised love, the law's delay,
The insolence of office, and the spurns
That patient merit of the unworthy takes,
When he himself might his quietus make
With a bare bodkin?

Here, out of 167 words, we find only 28 of foreign origin; and even these are Englished in their terminations or adjuncts. *Noble* is Norman-French; but the comparative *nobler* stamps it with the Teutonic mark. *Oppose* is Latin; but the participle *opposing* is true English. *Devout* is naturalised by the native adverbial termination, *devoutly*. *Oppressor's* and *despised* take English inflexions. The formative elements, *or, not, that, the, in, and, by, we,* and the rest, are all English. The only complete sentence which we could frame of wholly Latin words would be an imperative standing alone, as, "Observe," and even this would be English in form.

On the other hand, we may take the following passage from Mr. Herbert Spencer as a specimen of the largely Latinised vocabulary needed for expressing the exact ideas of science or philosophy. Here also borrowed words are printed in italics:—

"The *constitution* which we *assign* to this *etherial medium*, however, like the *constitution* we *assign* to *solid substance*, is *necessarily* an *abstract* of the *impressions received* from *tangible* bodies. The *opposition* to *pressure* which a *tangible* body *offers* to us is not shown in one *direction* only, but in all *directions*; and so likewise is its *tenacity. Suppose countless lines radiating* from its *centre* on every side, and it *resists* along each of these *lines* and *coheres* along each of these *lines*. Hence the *constitution* of those *ultimate units* through the *instrumentality* of which *phenomena* are *interpreted*. Be they *atoms* of *ponderable matter* or *molecules* of *ether*, the *properties* we *conceive* them to *possess* are nothing else than these *perceptible properties idealised.*"

In this case, out of 122 words we find no less than 46 are of foreign origin. Though this large proportion sufficiently shows the amount of our indebtedness to the classical languages for our abstract or specialised scientific terms, the absolutely indisputable nature of the English substratum remains clearly evident. The tongue which we use to-day is enriched by valuable loan words from many separate sources; but it is still as it has always been, English and nothing else. It is the self-same speech with the tongue of the Sleswick pirates and the West Saxon over-lords.

* * * * *

CHAPTER XIX.

ANGLO-SAXON NOMENCLATURE.

Perhaps nothing tends more to repel the modern English student from the early history of his country than the very unfamiliar appearance of the personal names which he meets before the Norman Conquest. There can be no doubt that such a shrinking from the first stages of our national annals does really exist; and it seems to be largely due to this very superficial and somewhat unphilosophical cause. Before the Norman invasion, the modern Englishman finds himself apparently among complete foreigners, in the Æthelwulfs, the Eadgyths, the Oswius, and the Seaxburhs of the Chronicle; while he hails the Norman invaders, the Johns, Henrys, Williams, and Roberts, of the period immediately succeeding the conquest, as familiar English friends. The contrast can scarcely be better given than in the story told about Æthelred's Norman wife. Her name was Ymma, or Emma; but the English of that time murmured against such an outlandish sound, and so the Lady received a new English name as Ælfgifu. At the present day our nomenclature has changed so utterly that Emma sounds like ordinary English, while Ælfgifu sounds like a wholly foreign word. The incidental light thrown upon our history by the careful study of personal names is indeed so valuable that a few remarks upon the subject seem necessary in order to complete our hasty survey of Anglo-Saxon Britain.

During the very earliest period when we catch a glimpse of the English people on the Continent or in eastern Britain, a double system of naming seems to have prevailed, not wholly unlike our modern plan of Christian and surname. The clan name was appended to the personal one. A man was apparently described as Wulf the Holting, or as Creoda the Æscing. The clan names were in many cases common to the English and the Continental Teutons. Thus we find Helsings in the English Helsington and the Swedish Helsingland; Harlings in the English Harlingham and the Frisian Harlingen; and Bleccings in the English Bletchingley and the Scandinavian Bleckingen. Our Thyrings at Thorrington answer, perhaps, to the Thuringians; our Myrgings at Merrington to the Frankish Merwings or Merovingians; our Wærings at Warrington to the Norse Væringjar or Varangians. At any rate, the clan organization was one common to both great branches of the Teutonic stock, and it has left its mark deeply upon our modern nomenclature, both in England and in Germany. Mr. Kemble has enumerated nearly 200 clan names found in early English charters and documents, besides over 600 others inferred from local names in England at the present day. Taking one letter of the alphabet alone, his list includes the Glæstings, Geddings, Gumenings, Gustings, Getings, Grundlings, Gildlings, and Gillings, from documentary evidence; and the Gærsings, Gestings, Geofonings, Goldings, and Garings, with many others, from the inferential evidence of existing towns and villages.

The personal names of the earliest period are in many cases untranslateable—that is to say, as with the first stratum of Greek names, they bear no obvious meaning in the language as we know it. Others are names of animals or natural objects. Unlike the later historical cognomens, they each consist, as a rule, of a single element, not of two elements in composition. Such are the names which we get in the narrative of the colonization and in the mythical genealogies; Hengest, Horsa, Æsc, Ælle, Cymen, Cissa, Bieda, Mægla; Ceol, Penda, Offa, Blecca; Esla, Gewis, Wig, Brand, and so forth. A few of these names (such as Penda and Offa), are undoubtedly historical; but of the rest, some seem to be etymological blunders, like Port and Wihtgar; others to be pure myths, like Wig and Brand; and others, again, to be doubtfully true, like Cerdic, Cissa, and

156

Bieda, eponyms, perhaps, of Cerdices-ford, Cissan-ceaster, and Biedan-heafod.

In the truly historical age, the clan system seems to have died out, and each person bore, as a rule, only a single personal name. These names are almost invariably compounded of two elements, and the elements thus employed were comparatively few in number. Thus, we get the root *æthel*, noble, as the first half in Æthelred, Æthelwulf, Æthelberht, Æthelstan, and Æthelbald. Again, the root *ead*, rich, or powerful, occurs in Eadgar, Eadred, Eadward, Eadwine, and Eadwulf. *Ælf*, an elf, forms the prime element in Ælfred, Ælfric, Ælfwine, Ælfward, and Ælfstan. These were the favourite names of the West-Saxon royal house; the Northumbrian kings seem rather to have affected the syllable *os*, divine, as in Oswald, Oswiu, Osric, Osred, and Oslaf. *Wine*, friend, is a favourite termination found in Æscwine, Eadwine, Æthelwine, Oswine, and Ælfwine, whose meanings need no further explanation. *Wulf* appears as the first half in Wulfstan, Wulfric, Wulfred, and Wulfhere; while it forms the second half in Æthelwulf, Eadwulf, Ealdwulf, and Cenwulf. *Beorht, berht*, or *briht*, bright, or glorious, appears in Beorhtric, Beorhtwulf, Brihtwald; Æthelberht, Ealdbriht, and Eadbyrht. *Burh*, a fortress, enters into many female names, as Eadburh, Æthelburh, Sexburh, and Wihtburh. As a rule, a certain number of syllables seem to have been regarded as proper elements for forming personal names, and to have been combined somewhat fancifully, without much regard to the resulting meaning. The following short list of such elements, in addition to the roots given above, will suffice to explain most of the names mentioned in this work.

- *Helm*: helmet.
- *Gar*: spear.
- *Gifu*: gift.
- *Here*: army.
- *Sige*: victory.
- *Cyne*: royal.

- *Leof*: dear.
- *Wig*: war.
- *Stan*: stone.
- *Eald*: old, venerable.
- *Weard, ward*: ward, protection.
- *Red*: counsel.
- *Eeg*: edge, sword.
- *Theod*: people, nation.

By combining these elements with those already given most of the royal or noble names in use in early England were obtained.

With the people, however, it would seem that shorter and older forms were still in vogue. The following document, the original of which is printed in Kemble's collection, represents the pedigree of a serf, and is interesting, both as showing the sort of names in use among the servile class, and the care with which their family relationships were recorded, in order to preserve the rights of their lord.

Dudda was a boor at Hatfield, and he had three daughters: one hight Deorwyn, the other Deorswith, the third Golde. And Wulflaf at Hatfield has Deorwyn to wife. Ælfstan, at Tatchingworth, has Deorswith to wife: and Ealhstan, Ælfstan's brother, has Golde to wife. There was a man hight Hwita, bee-master at Hatfield, and he had a daughter Tate, mother of Wulfsige, the bowman; and Wulfsige's sister Lulle has Hehstan to wife, at Walden. Wifus and Dunne and Seoloce are inborn at Hatfield. Duding, son of Wifus, lives at Walden; and Ceolmund, Dunne's son, also sits at Walden; and Æthelheah, Seoloce's son, also sits at Walden. And Tate, Cenwold's sister, Mæg has to wife at Welgun; and Eadhelm, Herethryth's son, has Tate's daughter to wife. Wærlaf, Wærstan's father, was a right serf at Hatfield; he kept the grey swine there.

In the west, and especially in Cornwall, the names of the serfs were mainly Celtic,—Griffith, Modred, Riol, and so forth,—as may be seen from the list of manumissions preserved in a mass-book at St. Petroc's, or Padstow. Elsewhere, however, the Celtic names seem to have dropped out, for the most part, with the Celtic language. It is true, we meet with cases of apparently Welsh forms, like Maccus, or Rum, even in purely Teutonic districts; and some names, such as Cerdic and Ceadwalla, seem to have been borrowed by one race from the other: while such forms as Wealtheow and Waltheof are at least suggestive of British descent: but on the whole, the conquered Britons appear everywhere to have quickly adopted the names in vogue among their conquerors. Such names would doubtless be considered fashionable, as was the case at a later date with those introduced by the Danes and the Normans. Even in Cornwall a good many English forms occur among the serfs: while in very Celtic Devonshire, English names were probably universal.

The Danish Conquest introduced a number of Scandinavian names, especially in the North, the consideration of which belongs rather to a companion volume. They must be briefly noted here, however, to prevent confusion with the genuine English forms. Amongst such Scandinavian introductions, the commonest are perhaps Harold, Swegen or Swend, Ulf, Gorm or Guthrum, Orm, Yric or Eric, Cnut, and Ulfcytel. During and after the time of the Danish dynasty, these forms, rendered fashionable by royal usage, became very general even among the native English. Thus Earl Godwine's sons bore Scandinavian names; and at an earlier period we even find persons, apparently Scandinavian, fighting on the English side against the Danes in East Anglia.

But the sequel to the Norman Conquest shows us most clearly how the whole nomenclature of a nation may be entirely altered without any large change of race. Immediately after the Conquest the native English names begin to disappear, and in their place we get a crop of Williams, Walters, Rogers, Henries, Ralphs, Richards, Gilberts, and Roberts. Most of these were originally High German forms, taken into Gaul by the

Franks, borrowed from them by the Normans, and then copied by the English from their foreign lords. A few, however, such as Arthur, Owen, and Alan, were Breton Welsh. Side by side with these French names, the Normans introduced the Scriptural forms, John, Matthew, Thomas, Simon, Stephen, Piers or Peter, and James; for though a few cases of Scriptural names occur in the earlier history—for example, St. John of Beverley and Daniel, bishop of the West Saxons—these are always borne by ecclesiastics, probably as names of religion. All through the middle ages, and down to very recent times, the vast majority of English men and women continued to bear these baptismal names of Norman introduction. Only two native English forms practically survived— Edward and Edmund—owing to mere accidents of royal favour. They were the names of two great English saints, Eadward the Confessor and Eadmund of East Anglia; and Henry III. bestowed them upon his two sons, Edward I. and Edmund of Lancaster. In this manner they became adopted into the royal and fashionable circle, and so were perpetuated to our own day. All the others died out in mediæval times, while the few old forms now current, such as Alfred, Edgar, Athelstane, and Edwin, are mere artificial revivals of the two last centuries. If we were to judge by nomenclature alone, we might almost fancy that the Norman Conquest had wholly extinguished the English people.

A few steps towards the adoption of surnames were taken even before the Conquest. Titles of office were usually placed after the personal name, as Ælfred King, Lilla Thegn, Wulfnoth Cild, Ælfward Bishop, Æthelberht Ealdorman, and Harold Earl. Double names occasionally occur, the second being a nickname or true surname, as Osgod Clapa, Benedict Biscop, Thurkytel Myranheafod, Godwine Bace, and Ælfric Cerm. Trade names are also found, as Ecceard smith, or Godwig boor. Everywhere, but especially in the Danish North, patronymics were in common use; for example, Harold Godwine's son, or Thored Gunnor's son. In all these cases we get surnames in the germ; but their general and official adoption dates from after the Norman Conquest.

Local nomenclature also demands a short explanation. Most of the Roman towns continued to be called by their Roman names: Londinium, Lunden, London; Eburacum, Eoforwic, Eurewic, York; Lindum Colonia, Lincolne, Lincoln. Often *ceaster*, from *castrum*, was added: Gwent, Venta Belgarum, Wintan-ceaster, Winteceaster, Winchester; Isca, Exan-ceaster, Execestre, Exeter; Corinium, Cyren-ceaster, Cirencester. Almost every place which is known to have had a name at the English Conquest retained that name afterwards, in a more or less clipped or altered form. Examples are Kent, Wight, Devon, Dorset; Manchester, Lancaster, Doncaster, Leicester, Gloucester, Worcester, Colchester, Silchester, Uttoxeter, Wroxeter, and Chester; Thames, Severn, Ouse, Don, Aire, Derwent, Swale, and Tyne. Even where the Roman name is now lost, as at Pevensey, the old form was retained in Early English days; for the "Chronicle" calls it Andredes-ceaster, that is to say, Anderida. So the old name of Bath is Akemannes-ceaster, derived from the Latin *Aqua*, Cissan-ceaster, Chichester, forms an almost solitary exception. Canterbury, or Cant-wara-byrig, was correctly known as Dwrovernum or Doroberna in Latin documents of the Anglo-Saxon period.

On the other hand, the true English towns which grew up around the strictly English settlements, bore names of three sorts. The first were the clan villages, the *hams* or *tuns*, such as Bænesingatun, Bensington; Snotingaham, Nottingham; Glæstingabyrig, Glastonbury; and Wæringwica, Warwick. These have already been sufficiently illustrated; and they were situated, for the most part, in the richest agricultural lowlands. The second were towns which grew up slowly for purposes of trade by fords of rivers or at ports: such are Oxeneford, Oxford; Bedcanford, Bedford (a British town); Stretford, Stratford; and Wealingaford, Wallingford. The third were the towns which grew up in the wastes and wealds, with names of varied form but more modern origin. As a whole, it may be said that during the entire early English period the names of cities were mostly Roman, the names of villages and country towns were mostly English.

* * * * *

CHAPTER XX.

ANGLO-SAXON LITERATURE.

Nothing better illustrates the original peculiarities and subsequent development of the early English mind than the Anglo-Saxon literature. A vast mass of manuscripts has been preserved for us, embracing works in prose and verse of the most varied kind; and all the most important of these have been made accessible to modern readers in printed copies. They cast a flood of light upon the workings of the English mind in all ages, from the old pagan period in Sleswick to the date of the Norman Conquest, and the subsequent gradual supplanting of our native literature by a new culture based upon the Romance models.

All national literature everywhere begins with rude songs. From the earliest period at which the English and Saxon people existed as separate tribes at all, we may be sure that they possessed battle-songs, like those common to the whole Aryan stock. But among the Teutonic races poetry was not distinguished by either of the peculiarities—rime or metre—which mark off modern verse from prose, so far as its external form is concerned. Our existing English system of versification is not derived from our old native poetry at all; it is a development of the Romance system, adopted by the school of Gower and Chaucer from the French and Italian poets. Its metre, or syllabic arrangement, is an adaptation from the Greek quantitative prosody, handed down through Latin and the neo-Latin dialects; its rime is a Celtic peculiarity borrowed by the Romance nationalities, and handed on through them to modern English literature by the Romance school of the fourteenth century. Our original English versification, on the other hand, was neither rimed nor rhythmic. What answered to metre was a certain irregular swing, produced by a roughly recurrent number of accents in each couplet, without restriction as to the number of feet or syllables. What answered to rime was a regular and marked alliteration, each couplet having a certain key-letter, with which three principal words in the couplet began. In addition to these two poetical devices, Anglo-Saxon verse shows traces of parallelism, similar to that which distinguishes Hebrew poetry. But the alliteration and parallelism do not run quite side by side, the second half of each alliterative couplet being parallel with the first half of the next couplet. Accordingly, each new sentence begins somewhat clumsily in the middle of the couplet. All these peculiarities are not, however, always to be distinguished in every separate poem.

The following rough translation of a very early Teutonic spell for the cure of a sprained ankle, belonging to the heathen period, will illustrate the earliest form of this alliterative verse. The key-letter in each couplet is printed in capitals, and the verse is read from end to end, not as two separate columns.[1]

Balder and Woden   Went to the Woodland:
There Balder's Foal   Fell, wrenching its Foot.
Then Sinthgunt beguiled him,   and Sunna her Sister:
Then Frua beguiled him,   and Folla her sister,
Then Woden beguiled him,   as Well he knew how;
Wrench of blood, Wrench of bone,   and eke Wrench of limb:
Bone unto Bone,   Blood unto Blood,
Limb unto Limb   as though Limèd it were.

In this simple spell the alliteration serves rather as an aid to memory than as an ornamental device. The following lines, translated from the ballad on Æthelstan's victory at Brunanburh, in 937, will show the developed form of the same versificatory system. The parallelism and alliteration are here well marked:—

Æthelstan king,   lord of Earls,
Bestower of Bracelets,   and his Brother eke,
Eadmund the Ætheling,   honour Eternal
Won in the Slaughter,   with edge of the Sword
By Brunnanbury.   The Bucklers they clave,
Hewed the Helmets   with Hammered steel,
Heirs of Edward,   as was their Heritage,
From their Fore-Fathers,   that oft the Field
They should Guard their Good folk   Gainst every comer,
Their Home and their Hoard.   The Hated foe cringed to them,
The Scottish Sailors,   and the Northern Shipmen;
Fated they Fell.   The Field lay gory
With Swordsmen's blood   Since the Sun rose
On Morning tide   a Mighty globe,
To Glide o'er the Ground,   God's candle bright,
The endless Lord's taper,   till the great Light
Sank to its Setting.   There Soldiers lay,
Warriors Wounded,   Northern Wights,
Shot over Shields;   and so Scotsmen eke,
Wearied with War.   The West Saxon onwards,
The Live-Long day   in Linkèd order
Followed the Footsteps   of the Foul Foe.

Of course no songs of the old heathen period were committed to writing either in Sleswick or in Britain. The minstrels who composed them taught them by word of mouth to their pupils, and so handed them down from generation to generation, much as the Achæan rhapsodists handed down the Homeric poems. Nevertheless, two or three such old songs were afterwards written out in Christian Northumbria or Wessex;

and though their heathendom has been greatly toned down by the transcribers, enough remains to give us a graphic glimpse of the fierce and gloomy old English nature which we could not otherwise obtain. One fragment, known as the *Fight at Finnesburh* (rescued from a book-cover into which it had been pasted), probably dates back before the colonisation of Britain, and closely resembles in style the above-quoted ode. Two other early pieces, the *Traveller's Song* and the *Lament of Deor*, are inserted from pagan tradition in a book of later devotional poems preserved at Exeter. But the great epic of *Beowulf*, a work composed when the English and the Danes were still living in close connexion with one another by the shores of the Baltic, has been handed down to us entire, thanks to the kind intervention of some Northumbrian monk, who, by Christianising the most flagrantly heathen portions, has saved the entire work from the fate which would otherwise have overtaken it. As a striking representation of early English life and thought, this great epic deserves a fuller description.[2]

Beowulf is written in the same short alliterative metre as that of the Brunanburh ballad, and takes its name from its hero, a servant or companion of the mighty Hygelac, king of the Geatas (Jutes or Goths). At a distance from his home lay the kingdom of the Scyldings, a Danish tribe, ruled over by Hrothgar. There stood Heorot, the high hall of heroes, the greatest mead-house ever raised. But the land of the Danes was haunted by a terrible fiend, known as Grendel, who dwelt in a dark fen in the forest belt, girt round with shadows and lit up at eve by flitting flames. Every night Grendel came forth and carried off some of the Danes to devour in his home. The description of the monster himself and of the marshland where he had his lair is full of that weird and gloomy superstition which everywhere darkens and overshadows the life of the savage and the heathen barbarian. The terror inspired in the rude English mind by the mark and the woodland, the home of wild beasts and of hostile ghosts, of deadly spirits and of fierce enemies, gleams luridly through every line. The fen and the forest are dim and dark; will-o'-the-wisps flit above them, and gloom closes them in; wolves and wild boars lurk there, the quagmire opens its jaws and swallows the horse and his rider; the foeman comes through it to bring fire and slaughter to the clan-village at the dead of night. To these real terrors and dangers of the mark are added the fancied ones of superstition. There the terrible forms begotten of man's vague dread of the unknown—elves and nickors and fiends—have their murky dwelling-place. The atmosphere of the strange old heathen epic is oppressive in its gloominess. Nevertheless, its poetry sometimes rises to a height of great, though barbaric, sublimity. Beowulf himself, hearing of the evil wrought by Grendel, set sail from his home for the land of the Danes. Hrothgar received him kindly, and entertained him and his Goths with ale and song in Heorot. Wealtheow, Hrothgar's queen, gold-decked, served them with mead. But when all had retired to rest on the couches of the great hall, in the murky night, Grendel came. He seized and slew one of Beowulf's companions. Then the warrior of the Goths followed the monster, and wounded him sorely with his hands. Grendel fled to his lair to die. But after the contest, Grendel's mother, a no less hateful creature—the "Devil's dam" of our mediæval legends—carries on the war against the slayer of her son. Beowulf descends to her home beneath the water, grapples with her in her cave, turns against her the weapons he finds there, and is again victorious. The Goths return to their own country laden with gifts by Hrothgar. After the death of Hygelac, Beowulf succeeds to the kingship of the Geatas, whom he rules well and prosperously for many years. At length a mysterious being, named the Fire Drake, a sort of dragon guarding a hidden treasure, some of which has been stolen while its guardian sleeps, comes out to slaughter his people. The old hero buckles on his rune-covered sword again, and goes forth to battle with the monster. He slays it, indeed, but is blasted by its fiery breath, and dies after the encounter. His companions light his pyre upon a lofty spit of land jutting out into the winter sea. Weapons and jewels and drinking bowls, taken from the Fire Drake's treasure, were thrown into the tomb for the use of the ghost in the other world; and a mighty barrow was raised upon the spot to be a beacon far and wide to seafaring men. So ends the great heathen epic. It gives us the most valuable picture which we possess of the daily life led by our pagan forefathers.

But though these poems are the oldest in tone, they are not the oldest in form of all that we possess. It is probable that the most primitive Anglo-Saxon verse was identical with prose, and consisted merely of sentences bound together by parallelism. As alliteration, at first a mere *memoria technica*, became an ornamental adjunct, and grew more developed, the parallelism gradually dropped out. Gnomes or short proverbs of this character were in common use, and they closely resembled the mediæval proverbs current in England to the present day.

With the introduction of Christianity, English verse took a new direction. It was chiefly occupied in devotional and sacred poetry, or rather, such poems only have come down to us, as the monks transcribed them alone, leaving the half-heathen war-songs of the minstrels attached to the great houses to die out unwritten. The first piece of English literature which we can actually date is a fragment of the great religious epic of Cædmon, written about the year 670. Cædmon was a poor brother in Hild's monastery at Whitby, and he acquired the art of poetry by a miracle. Northumbria, in the sixth and seventh centuries, took the lead in Teutonic Britain; and all the early literature is Northumbrian, as all the later literature is West Saxon. Cædmon's poem consisted in a paraphrase of the Bible history, from the Creation to the Ascension. The idea of a translation of the Bible from Latin into English would never have occurred to any one at that early time. English had as yet no literary form into which it could be thrown. But Cædmon conceived the notion of paraphrasing the Bible story in the old alliterative Teutonic verse, which was familiar to his hearers in songs like *Beowulf*. Some of the brethren translated or interpreted for him portions of the Vulgate, and he threw them into rude metre. Only a single short excerpt has come down to us in the original form. There is a later complete epic, however, also attributed to Cædmon, of the same scope and purport; and it retains so much of the old heathen spirit that it may very possibly represent a modernised version of the real Cædmon's poem, by a reviser in the ninth century. At any rate, the latter work may be treated here under the name of Cædmon, by which it is universally known. It consists of a long Scriptural paraphrase, written in the alliterative metre, short, sharp, and decisive, but not without a wild and passionate beauty of its own. In tone it differs wonderfully little from *Beowulf*, being most at home in the war of heaven and Satan, and in the titanic descriptions of the devils and their deeds. The conduct of the poem is singularly like that of *Paradise Lost*. Its wild and rapid stanzas show how little Christianity had yet moulded the barbaric nature of the newly-converted English. The epic is essentially a war-song; the Hebrew element is far stronger than the Christian; hell takes the place of Grendel's mere; and, to borrow Mr. Green's admirable phrase, "the verses fall like sword-strokes in the thick of battle."

In all these works we get the genuine native English note, the wild song of a pirate race, shaped in early minstrelsy for celebrating the deeds of gods and warriors, and scarcely half-adapted afterward to the not wholly alien tone of the oldest Hebrew Scriptures. But the Latin schools, set up by the Italian monks, introduced into England a totally new and highly-developed literature. The pagan Anglo-Saxons had not advanced beyond the stage of ballads; they had no history, or other prose literature of their own, except, perhaps, a few traditional genealogical lists, mostly mythical, and adapted to an artificial grouping by eights and forties. The Roman missionaries brought over the Roman works, with their developed historical and philosophical style; and the change induced in England by copying these originals was as great as the change would now be from the rude Polynesian myths and ballads to a history of Polynesia written in English, and after English prototypes, by a native convert. In fact, the Latin language was almost as important to the new departure as the Latin models. While the old English literary form, restricted entirely to poetry, was unfitted for any serious narrative or any reflective work, the

168

old English tongue, suited only to the practical needs of a rude warrior race, was unfitted for the expression of any but the simplest and most material ideas. It is true, the vocabulary was copious, especially in terms for natural objects, and it was far richer than might be expected even in words referring to mental states and emotions; but in the expression of abstract ideas, and in idioms suitable for philosophical discussion, it remained still, of course, very deficient. Hence the new serious literature was necessarily written entirely in the Latin language, which alone possessed the words and modes of speech fitted for its development; but to exclude it on that account from the consideration of Anglo-Saxon literature, as many writers have done, would be an absurd affectation. The Latin writings of Englishmen are an integral part of English thought, and an important factor in the evolution of English culture. Gradually, as English monks grew to read Latin from generation to generation, they invented corresponding compounds in their own language for the abstract words of the southern tongue; and therefore by the beginning of the eleventh century, the West Saxon speech of Ælfred and his successors had grown into a comparatively wealthy dialect, suitable for the expression of many ideas unfamiliar to the rude pirates and farmers of Sleswick and East Anglia. Thus, in later days, a rich vernacular literature grew up with many distinct branches. But, in the earlier period, the use of a civilised idiom for all purposes connected with the higher civilisation introduced by the missionaries was absolutely necessary; and so we find the codes of laws, the penitentials of the Church, the charters, and the prose literature generally, almost all written at first in Latin alone. Gradually, as the English tongue grew fuller, we find it creeping into use for one after another of these purposes; but to the last an educated Anglo-Saxon could express himself far more accurately and philosophically in the cultivated tongue of Rome than in the rough dialect of his Teutonic countrymen. We have only to contrast the bald and meagre style of the "English Chronicle," written in the mother-tongue, with the fulness and ease of Bæda's "Ecclesiastical History," written two centuries earlier in Latin, in order to see how great an advantage the rough Northumbrians of the early Christian period obtained in the gift of an old and polished instrument for conveying to one another their higher thoughts.

Of this new literature (which began with the Latin biography of Wilfrith by Æddi or Eddius, and the Latin verses of Ealdhelm) the great representative is, in fact, Bæda, whose life has already been sufficiently described in an earlier chapter. Living at Jarrow, a Benedictine monastery of the strictest type, in close connection with Rome, and supplied with Roman works in abundance, Bæda had thoroughly imbibed the spirit of the southern culture, and his books reflect for us a true picture of the English barbarian toned down and almost obliterated in all distinctive features by receptivity for Italian civilisation. The Northumbrian kingdom had just passed its prime in his days; and he was able to record the early history of the English Church and People with something like Roman breadth of view. His scientific knowledge was up to that of his contemporaries abroad; while his somewhat childish tales of miracles and visions, though they often betray traces of the old heathen spirit, were not below the average level of European thought in his own day. Altogether, Bæda may be taken as a fair specimen of the Romanised Englishman, alike in his strength and in his weakness. The samples of his historical style already given will suffice for illustration of his Latin works; but it must not be forgotten that he was also one of the first writers to try his hand at regular English prose in his translation of St. John's Gospel. A few English verses from his lips have also come down to us, breathing the old Teutonic spirit more deeply than might be expected from his other works.

During the interval between the Northumbrian and West Saxon supremacies—the interval embraced by the eighth century, and covered by the greatness of Mercia under Æthelbald and Offa—we have few remains of English literature. The laws of Ine the West Saxon, and of Offa the Mercian, with the Penitentials of the Church, and the Charters, form the chief documents. But England gained no little credit for learning from the works of two Englishmen who had taken up their abode in the old Germanic kingdom: Boniface or Winfrith, the apostle of the heathen Teutons subjugated by the Franks, and Alcuin (Ealhwine), the famous friend and secretary of Karl the Great. Many devotional Anglo-Saxon poems, of various dates, are kept for us in the two books preserved at Exeter, and at Vercelli in North Italy. Amongst them are some by Cynewulf, perhaps the most genuinely poetical of all the early minstrels after Cædmon. The following lines, taken from the beginning of his poem "The Phœnix" (a transcript from Lactantius), will sufficiently illustrate his style:—

I have heard that hidden
On the east of earth
Lovely and famous.
May not be reached
Dwellers on earth;
Through the might of the Maker
Fair is the field,
Filled with the sweetest
Unique is that island,
Mickle of might
There oft lieth open
With happiest harmony,
Winsome its woods
Roomy with reaches.
Nor breath of frost,
Nor summer's heat,
Nor fall of hail,
Nor weltering weather,
Falleth on any;
Ever in peace,
Bloometh with blossoms.
Standeth not steep,

Afar from hence
Is a fairest isle,
The lap of that land
By many mortals,
But it is divided
From all misdoers.
Full happy and glad,
Scented flowers.
Almighty the worker
Who moulded that land.
To the eyes of the blest,
The gate of heaven.
And its fair green wolds,
No rain there nor snow,
Nor fiery blast,
Nor scattered sleet,
Nor hoary rime,
Nor wintry shower,
But the field resteth
And the princely land
Berg there nor mount
Nor stony crag

High lifteth the head,	As here with us,
Nor vale, nor dale,	Nor deep-caverned down,
Hollows or hills;	Nor hangeth aloft
Aught of unsmooth;	But ever the plain,
Basks in the beam,	Joyfully blooming.
Twelve fathoms taller	Towereth that land
(As quoth in their writs	Many wise men)
Than ever a berg	That bright among mortals
High lifteth the head	Among heaven's stars.

Two noteworthy points may be marked in this extract. Its feeling for natural scenery is quite different from the wild sublimity of the descriptions of nature in *Beowulf*. Cynewulf's verse is essentially the verse of an agriculturist; it looks with disfavour upon mountains and rugged scenes, while its ideal is one of peaceful tillage. The monk speaks out in it as cultivator and dreamer. Its tone is wholly different from that of the Brunanburh ballad or the other fierce war-songs. Moreover, it contains one or two rimes, preserved in this translation, whose full significance will be pointed out hereafter.

The anarchy of Northumbria, and still more the Danish inroads, put an end to the literary movement in the North and the Midlands; but the struggle in Wessex gave new life to the West Saxon people. Under Ælfred, Winchester became the centre of English thought. But the West Saxon literature is almost entirely written in English, not in Latin; a fact which marks the progressive development of vocabulary and idiom in the native tongue. Ælfred himself did much to encourage literature, inviting over learned men from the continent, and founding schools for the West Saxon youth in his dwarfed dominions. Most of the Winchester works are attributed to his own pen, though doubtless he was largely aided by his advisers, and amongst others by Asser, his Welsh secretary and Bishop of Sherborne. They comprise translations into the Anglo-Saxon of Boëthius *de Consolatione*, the Universal History of Orosius, Bæda's Ecclesiastical

History, and Pope Gregory's *Regula Pastoralis*. But the fact that Ælfred still has recourse to Roman originals, marks the stage of civilisation as yet mainly imitative; while the interesting passages intercalated by the king himself show that the beginnings of a really native prose literature were already taking shape in English hands.

The chief monument of this truly Anglo-Saxon literature, begun and completed by English writers in the English tongue alone, is the Chronicle. That invaluable document, the oldest history of any Teutonic race in its own language, was probably first compiled at the court of Ælfred. Its earlier part consists of mere royal genealogies of the first West Saxon kings, together with a few traditions of the colonisation, and some excerpts from Bæda. But with the reign of Æthelwulf, Ælfred's father, it becomes comparatively copious, though its records still remain dry and matter-of-fact, a bare statement of facts, without comment or emotional display. The following extract, giving the account of Ælfred's death, will show its meagre nature. The passage has been modernised as little as is consistent with its intelligibility at the present day:—

An. 901. Here died Ælfred Æthulfing [Æthelwulfing—the son of Æthelwulf], six nights ere All Hallow Mass. He was king over all English-kin, bar that deal that was under Danish weald [dominion]; and he held that kingdom three half-years less than thirty winters. There came Eadward his son to the rule. And there seized Æthelwold ætheling, his father's brother's son, the ham [villa] at Winburne [Wimbourne], and at Tweoxneam [Christchurch], by the king's unthank and his witan's [without leave from the king]. There rode the king with his fyrd till he reached Badbury against Winburne. And Æthelwold sat within the ham, with the men that to him had bowed, and he had forwrought [obstructed] all the gates in, and said that he would either there live or there lie. Thereupon rode the ætheling on night away, and sought the [Danish] host in Northumbria, and they took him for king and bowed to him.

And the king bade ride after him, but they could not outride him. Then beset man the woman that he had erst taken without the king's leave, and against the bishop's word, for that she was ere that hallowed a nun. And on this ilk year forth-fared Æthelred (he was ealdorman on Devon) four weeks ere Ælfred king.

During the Augustan age the Chronicle grows less full, but contains several fine war-songs, of the genuine old English type, full of savagery in sentiment, and abrupt or broken in manner, but marked by the same wild poetry and harsh inversions as the older heathen ballads. Amongst them stand the lines on the fight of Brunanburh, whose exordium is quoted above. Its close forms one of the finest passages in old English verse:—

Behind them they Left, the Lych to devour,
The Sallow kite and the Swart raven,
Horny of beak,— and Him, the dusk-coated,
The white-afted Erne, the corse to Enjoy,
The Greedy war-hawk, and that Grey beast,
The Wolf of the Wood. No such Woeful slaughter
Aye on this Island Ever hath been,
By edge of the Sword, as book Sayeth,
Writers of Eld, since of Eastward hither
English and Saxons Sailed over Sea,
O'er the Broad Brine,— landed in Britain,
Proud Workers of War, and o'ercame the Welsh,
Earls Eager of fame, Obtaining this Earth.

During the decadence, in the disastrous reign of Æthelred, the Chronicle regains its fulness, and the following passage may be taken as a good specimen of its later style. It shows the approach to comment and reflection, as the compilers grew more accustomed to historical writing in their own tongue:—

An. 1009. Here on this year were the ships ready of which we ere spake, and there were so many of them as never ere (so far as books tell us) were made among English kin in no king's day. And man brought them all together to Sandwich, and there should they lie, and hold this earth against all outlanders [foreigners'] hosts. But we had not yet the luck nor the worship [valour] that the ship-fyrd should be of any good to this land, no more than it oft was afore. Then befel it at this ilk time or a little ere, that Brihtric, Eadric's brother the ealdorman's, forwrayed [accused] Wulfnoth child to the king: and he went out and drew unto him twenty ships, and there harried everywhere by the south shore, and wrought all evil. Then quoth man to the ship-fyrd that man might easily take them, if man were about it. Then took Brihtric to himself eighty ships and thought that he should work himself great fame if he should get Wulfnoth, quick or dead. But as they were thitherward, there came such a wind against them such as no man ere minded [remembered], and it all to-beat and to-brake the ships, and warped them on land: and soon came Wulfnoth and for-burned the ships. When this was couth [known] to the other ships where the king was, how the others fared, then was it as though it were all redeless, and the king fared him home, and the ealdormen, and the high witan, and forlet the ships thus lightly. And the folk that were on the ships brought them round eft to Lunden, and let all the people's toil thus lightly go for nought: and the victory that all English kin hoped for was no better. There this ship-fyrd was thus ended; then came, soon after Lammas, the huge foreign host, that we hight Thurkill's host, to Sandwich, and soon wended their way to Canterbury, and would quickly have won the burg if they had not rather yearned for peace of them. And all the East Kentings made peace with the host, and gave it three thousand pound. And the host there, soon after that, wended till it came to Wightland, and there everywhere in Suth-Sex, and on Hamtunshire, and eke on Berkshire harried and burnt, as their wont is. Then bade the king call out all the people, that men should hold against them on every half [side]: but none the less, look! they fared where they willed. Then one time had the king foregone before them with all the fyrd as they were going to their ships, and all the folk was ready to fight them. But it was let, through Eadric ealdorman, as it ever yet was. Then, after St. Martin's mass, they fared eft again into Kent, and took them a winter seat on Thames, and victualled themselves from East-Sex and from the shires that there next were, on the twain halves of Thames. And oft they fought against the burg of Lunden, but praise be to God, it yet stands sound, and they ever there fared evilly. And there after mid-winter they took their way up, out through Chiltern, and so to Oxenaford [Oxford], and for-burnt the burg, and took their way on to the twa halves of Thames to shipward. There man warned them that there was fyrd gathered at Lunden against them; then wended they over at Stane [Staines]. And thus fared they all the winter, and that Lent were in Kent and bettered [repaired] their ships.

We possess several manuscript versions of the Chronicle, belonging to different abbeys, and containing in places somewhat different accounts. Thus the Peterborough copy is fullest on matters affecting that monastery, and even inserts several spurious grants, which, however, are of value as showing how incapable the writers were of scientific forgery, and so as guarantees of the general accuracy of the document. But in the main facts they all agree. Nor do they stop short at the Norman Conquest. Most of them continue half through the reign of William, and then cease; while one manuscript goes on uninterruptedly till the reign of Stephen, and breaks off abruptly in the year 1154 with an unfinished sentence. With it, native prose literature dies down altogether until the reign of Edward III.

As a whole, however, the Conquest struck the death-blow of Anglo-Saxon literature almost at once. During the reigns of Ælfred's descendants Wessex had produced a rich crop of native works on all subjects, but especially religious. In this literature the greatest name was that of Ælfric, whose Homilies are models of the classical West Saxon prose. But after the Conquest our native literature died out wholly, and a new literature, founded on Romance models, took its place. The Anglo-Saxon style lingered on among the people, but it was gradually killed down by the Romance style of the court writers. In prose, the history of William of Malmesbury, written in Latin, and in a wider continental spirit, marks the change. In poetry, the English school struggled on longer, but at last succumbed. A few words on the nature of this process will not be thrown away.

The old Teutonic poetry, with its treble system of accent, alliteration, and parallelism, was wholly different from the Romance poetry, with its double system of rime and metre. But, from an early date, the English themselves were fond of verbal jingles, such as "Scot and lot," "sac and soc," "frith and grith," "eorl and ceorl," or "might and right." Even in the alliterative poems we find many occasional rimes, such as "hlynede and dynede," "wide and side," "Dryht-guman sine drencte mid wine," or such as the rimes already quoted from Cynewulf. As time went on, and intercourse with other countries became greater, the tendency to rime settled down into a fixed habit. Rimed Latin verse was already familiar to the clergy, and was imitated in their works. Much of the very ornate Anglo-Saxon prose of the latest period is full of strange verbal tricks, as shown in the following modernised extract from a sermon of Wulfstan. Here, the alliterative letters are printed in capitals, and the rimes in italics:—

No Wonder is it that Woes befall us, for Well We Wot that now full many a year men little *care* what thing they *dare* in word or deed; and Sorely has this nation Sinned, whate'er man Say, with Manifold Sins and with right Manifold Misdeeds, with Slayings and with Slaughters, with *robbing* and with *stabbing*, with Grasping *deed* and hungry *Greed*, through Christian Treason and through heathen Treachery, through *guile* and through *wile*, through *lawlessness* and *awelessness*, through Murder of Friends and Murder of Foes, through broken Troth and broken Truth, through wedded unchastity and cloistered impurity. Little they *trow* of marriage *vow*, as ere this I said: little they reck the breach of *oath* or *troth*; swearing and forswearing, on every *side*, far and *wide*, Fast and Feast they hold not, Peace and Pact they keep not, oft and anon. Thus in this *land* they *stand*, Foes to Christendom, Friends to heathendom, Persecutors of Priests, Persecutors of People, all too many; spurners of godly law and Christian bond, who Loudly Laugh at the *Teaching* of God's *Teachers* and the *Preaching* of God's *Preachers*, and whatso rightly to God's rites belongs.

The nation was thus clearly preparing itself from within for the adoption of the Romance system. Immediately after the Conquest, rimes begin to appear distinctly, while alliteration begins to die out. An Anglo-Saxon poem on the character of William the Conqueror, inserted in the Chronicle under the year of his death, consists of very rude rimes which may be modernised as follows—

> Gold he took by might,
> And of great unright,
> From his folk with evil deed
> For sore little need.
> He was on greediness befallen,
> And getsomeness he loved withal.
> He set a mickle deer frith,
> And he laid laws therewith,

That whoso slew hart or hind
Him should man then blinden.
He forbade to slay the harts,
And so eke the boars.
So well he loved the high deer
As if he their father were.
Eke he set by the hares
That they might freely fare.
His rich men mourned it
And the poor men wailed it.
But he was so firmly wrought
That he recked of all nought.
And they must all withal
The king's will follow,
If they wished to live
Or their land have,
Or their goods eke,
Or his peace to seek.
Woe is me,
That any man so proud should be,
Thus himself up to raise,
And over all men to boast.
May God Almighty show his soul mild-heart-ness,
And do him for his sins forgiveness!

From that time English poetry bifurcates. On the one hand, we have the survival of the old Teutonic alliterative swing in Layamon's Brut and in Piers Plowman—the native verse of the people sung by native minstrels: and on the other hand we have the new Romance rimed metre in Robert of Gloucester, "William of Palerne," Gower, and Chaucer. But from Piers Plowman and Chaucer onward the Romance system conquers and the Teutonic system dies rapidly. Our modern poetry is wholly Romance in descent, form, and spirit.

Thus in literature as in civilisation generally, the culture of old Rome, either as handed down ecclesiastically through the Latin, or as handed down popularly through the Norman-French, overcame the native Anglo-Saxon culture, such as it was, and drove it utterly out of the England which we now know. Though a new literature, in Latin and English, sprang up after the Conquest, that literature had its roots, not in Sleswick or in Wessex, but in Greece, in Rome, in Provence, and in Normandy. With the Normans, a new era began—an era when Romance civilisation was grafted by harsh but strong hands on to the Anglo-Saxon stock, the Anglo-Saxon institutions, and the Anglo-Saxon tongue. With the first step in this revolution, our present volume has completed its assigned task. The story of the Normans will be told by another pen in the same series.

1. The original of this heathen charm is in the Old High German dialect; but it is quoted here as a good specimen of the early form of alliterative verse. A similar charm undoubtedly existed in Anglo-Saxon, though no copy of it has come down to our days, as we possess a modernised and Christianised English version, in which the name of our Lord is substituted for that of Balder.
2. It is right to state, however, that many scholars regard *Beowulf* as a late translation from a Danish original.

* * * * *

CHAPTER XXI.

ANGLO-SAXON INFLUENCES IN
MODERN BRITAIN.

Perhaps the best way of summing up the results of the present inquiry will be by considering briefly the main elements of our existing life and our actual empire which we owe to the Anglo-Saxon nationality. We may most easily glance at them under the five separate heads of blood, character, language, civilisation, and institutions.

In *blood*, it is probable that the importance of the Anglo-Saxon element has been generally over-estimated. It has been too usual to speak of England as though it were synonymous with Britain, and to overlook the numerical strength of the Celtic population in Scotland, Wales, Cornwall, and Ireland. It has been too usual, also, to neglect the considerable Danish, Norwegian, and Norman element, which, though belonging to the same Low German and Scandinavian stock, yet differs in some important particulars from the Anglo-Saxon. But we have seen reason to conclude that even in the most purely Teutonic region of Britain, the district between Forth and Southampton Water, a considerable proportion of the people were of Celtic or pre-Celtic descent, from the very first age of English settlement. This conclusion is borne out both by the physical traits of the peasantry and the nature of the early remains. In the western half of South Britain, from Clyde to Cornwall, the proportion of Anglo-Saxon blood has probably always been far smaller. The Norman conquerors themselves were of mixed Scandinavian, Gaulish, and Breton descent.

Throughout the middle ages, the more Teutonic half of Britain—the southern and eastern tract—was undoubtedly the most important: and the English, mixed with Scandinavians from Denmark or Normandy, formed the ruling caste. Up to the days of Elizabeth, Teutonic Britain led the van in civilisation, population, and commerce. But since the age of the Tudors, it seems probable, as Dr. Rolleston and others have shown, that the Celtic element has largely reasserted itself. A return wave of Celts has inundated the Teutonic region. Scottish Highlanders have poured into Glasgow, Edinburgh, and London: Welshmen have poured into Liverpool, Manchester, and all the great towns of England: Irishmen have poured into every part of the British dominions. During the middle ages, the Teutonic portion of Britain was by far the most densely populated; but at the present day, the almost complete restriction of coal to the Celtic or semi-Celtic area has aggregated the greatest masses of population in the west and north. If we take into consideration the probable large substratum of Celts or earlier races in the Teutonic counties, the wide area of the undoubted Celtic region which pours forth a constant stream of emigrants towards the Teutonic tract, the change of importance between south-east and north-west, since the industrial development of the coal country, and the more rapid rate of increase among the Celts, it becomes highly probable that not one-half the population of the British Isles is really of Teutonic descent. Moreover, it must be remembered that, whatever may have been the case in the primitive Anglo-Saxon period, intermarriages between Celts and Teutons have been common for at least four centuries past; and that therefore almost all Englishmen at the present day possess at least a fraction of Celtic blood.

"The people," says Professor Huxley, "are vastly less Teutonic than their language." It is not likely that any absolutely pure-blooded Anglo-Saxons now exist in our midst at all, except perhaps among the farmer class in the most Teutonic and agricultural shires: and even this exception is extremely doubtful. Persons bearing the most obviously Celtic names—Welsh, Cornish, Irish, or Highland Scots—are to be found in all our large towns, and scattered up and down through the country districts. Hence we may conclude with great probability that the Anglo-Saxon blood has long since been everywhere diluted by a strong Celtic intermixture. Even in the earliest times and in the most Teutonic counties, many serfs of non-Teutonic race existed from the very beginning: their masters have ere now mixed with other non-Teutonic families elsewhere, till even the restricted English people at the present day can hardly claim to be much more than half Anglo-Saxon. Nor do the Teutons now even retain their position as a ruling caste. Mixed Celts in England itself have long since risen to many high places. Leading families of Welsh, Cornish, Scotch, and Irish blood have also been admitted into the peerage of the United Kingdom, and form a large proportion of the House of Commons, of the official world, and of the governing class in India, the Colonies, and the empire generally. These families have again intermarried with the nobility and gentry of English, Danish, or Norman extraction, and thus have added their part to the intricate intermixture of the two races. At the present day, we can only speak of the British people as Anglo-Saxons in a conventional sense: so far as blood goes, we need hardly hesitate to set them down as a pretty equal admixture of Teutonic and Celtic elements.

In *character*, the Anglo-Saxons have bequeathed to us much of the German solidity, industry, and patience, traits which have been largely amalgamated with the intellectual quickness and emotional nature of the Celt, and have thus produced the prevailing English temperament as we actually know it. To the Anglo-Saxon blood we may doubtless attribute our general sobriety, steadiness, and persistence; our scientific patience and thoroughness; our political moderation and endurance; our marked love of individual freedom and impatience of arbitrary restraint. The Anglo-Saxon was slow to learn, but retentive of what he learnt. On the other hand, he was unimaginative; and this want of imagination may be traced in the more Teutonic counties to the present day. But when these qualities have been counteracted by the Celtic wealth of fancy, the race has produced the great English literature,—a literature whose form is wholly Roman, while in matter, its more solid parts doubtless owe much to the Teuton, and its lighter portions, especially its poetry and romance, can be definitely traced in great measure to known Celtic elements. While the Teutonic blood differentiates our somewhat slow and steady character from the more logical but volatile and unstable Gaul, the Celtic blood differentiates it from the far slower, heavier, and less quick or less imaginative Teutons of Germany and Scandinavia.

In *language* we owe almost everything to the Anglo-Saxons. The Low German dialect which they brought with them from Sleswick and Hanover still remains in all essentials the identical speech employed by ourselves at the present day. It received a few grammatical forms from the cognate Scandinavian dialects; it borrowed a few score or so of words from the Welsh; it adopted a small Latin vocabulary of ecclesiastical terms from the early missionaries; it took in a considerable number of Romance elements after the Norman Conquest; it enriched itself with an immense variety of learned compounds from the Greek and Latin at the Renaissance period: but all these additions affected almost exclusively its stock of words, and did not in the least interfere with its structure or its place in the scientific classification of languages. The English which we now speak is not in any sense a Romance tongue. It is the lineal descendant of the English of Ælfred and of Bæda, enlarged in its vocabulary by many words which they did not use, impoverished by the loss of a few which they employed, yet still essentially identical in grammar and idiom with the language of the first Teutonic settlers. Gradually losing its inflexions from the days of Eadgar onward, it assumed its existing type before the thirteenth century, and continuously incorporated an immense number of French and Latin words, which greatly increased its value as an instrument of thought. But it is important to recollect that the English tongue has nothing at all to do in its origin with either Welsh or French. The Teutonic speech of the Anglo-Saxon settlers drove out the old Celtic speech throughout almost all England and the Scotch Lowlands before the end of the eleventh century; it drove out the Cornish in the eighteenth century; and it is now driving out the Welsh, the Erse, and the Gaelic, under our very eyes. In language at least the British empire (save of course India) is now almost entirely English, or in other words, Anglo-Saxon.

In *civilisation*, on the other hand, we owe comparatively little to the direct Teutonic influence. The native Anglo-Saxon culture was low, and even before its transplantation to Britain it had undergone some modification by mediate mercantile transactions with Rome and the Mediterranean states. The alphabet, coins, and even a few southern words, (such as "alms") had already filtered through to the shores of the Baltic. After the colonisation of Britain, the Anglo-Saxons learnt something of the higher agriculture from their Romanised serfs, and adopted, as early as the heathen period, some small portion of the Roman system, so far as regarded roads, fortifications, and, perhaps buildings. The Roman towns still stood in their midst, and a fragment, at least, of the Romanised population still carried on commerce with the half-Roman Frankish kingdom across the Channel. The re-introduction of Christianity was at the same time the re-introduction of Roman culture in its later form. The Latin language and the Mediterranean arts once more took their place in Britain. The Romanising prelates,—Wilfrith, Theodore, Dunstan,—were also the leaders of civilisation in their own times. The Norman Conquest brought England into yet closer connection with the Continent; and Roman law and Roman arts still more deeply affected our native culture. Norman artificers supplanted the rude English handicraftsmen in many cases, and became a dominant class in towns. The old English literature, and especially the old English poetry, died utterly out with Piers Plowman; while a new literature, based upon Romance models, took its origin with Chaucer and the other Court poets. Celtic-Latin rhyme ousted the genuine Teutonic alliteration. With the Renaissance, the triumph of the southern culture was complete. Greek philosophy and Greek science formed the starting-point for our modern developments. The ecclesiastical revolt from papal Rome was accompanied by a literary and artistic return to the models of pagan Rome. The Renaissance was, in fact, the throwing off of all that was Teutonic and mediæval, the resumption of progressive thought and scientific knowledge, at the point where it had been interrupted by the Germanic inroads of the fifth century. The unjaded vigour of the German races, indeed, counted for much; and Europe took up the lost thread of the dying empire with a youthful freshness very different from the effete listlessness of the Mediterranean culture in its last stage. Yet it is none the less true that our whole civilisation is even now the carrying out and completion of the Greek and Roman culture in new fields and with fresh intellects. We owe little here to the Anglo-Saxon; we owe everything to the great stream of western culture, which began in Egypt and Assyria, permeated Greece and the Archipelago, spread to Italy and the Roman empire, and, finally, now embraces the whole European and American world. The Teutonic intellect and the Teutonic character have largely modified the spirit of the Mediterranean civilisation; but the tools, the instruments, the processes themselves, are all legacies from a different race. Englishmen did not invent letters, money, metallurgy, glass, architecture, and science; they received them all ready-made, from Italy and the Ægean, or more remotely still from the Euphrates and the Nile. Nor is it necessary to add that in religion we have no debt to the Anglo-Saxon, our existing creed being entirely derived through Rome from the Semitic race.

In *institutions*, once more, the Anglo-Saxon has contributed almost everything. Our political government, our limited monarchy, our parliament, our shires, our hundreds, our townships, are considered by the dominant school of historians to be all Anglo-Saxon in origin. Our jury is derived from an Anglo-Saxon custom; our nobility and officials are representatives of Anglo-Saxon earls and reeves. The Teuton, when he settled in Britain, brought with him the Teutonic organisation in its entirety. He established it throughout the whole territory which he occupied or conquered. As the West Saxon over-lordship grew to be the English kingdom, and as the English kingdom gradually annexed or coalesced with the Welsh and Cornish principalities, the Scotch and Irish kingdoms,—the Teutonic system spread over the whole of Britain. It underwent some little modification at the hands of the Normans, and more still at those of the Angevins; but, on the whole, it is still a wide yet natural development of the old Germanic constitution.

Thus, to sum up in a single sentence, the Anglo-Saxons have contributed about one-half the blood of Britain, or rather less; but they have contributed the whole framework of the language, and the whole social and political organisation; while, on the other hand, they have contributed hardly any of the civilisation, and none of the religion. We are now a mixed race, almost equally Celtic and Teutonic by descent; we speak a purely Teutonic language, with a large admixture of Latin roots in its vocabulary; we live under Teutonic institutions; we enjoy the fruits of a Græco-Roman civilisation; and we possess a Christian Church, handed down to us directly through Roman sources from a Hebrew original. To the extent so indicated, and to that extent only, we may still be justly styled an Anglo-Saxon people.

* * * * *

THE END.

Milton Keynes UK
Ingram Content Group UK Ltd.
UKHW022235280723
425995UK00004B/142

9 781017 867459